In La...

T0155126

In Later Years

Finding Meaning and Spirit in Aging

Bruce T. Marshall

Skinner House Books
Boston

Contents

Introduction

"I don't belong here!"

A visceral response rose in me as I entered the senior residence community where I had been hired to serve as a chaplain. My eyes were drawn to a thin frail woman steadying herself with a walker. She seemed to need all the attention she could gather to take one careful step, then another, then another.

An overweight man who appeared to have been poured into a motorized wheelchair drove by, acknowledging no one, a fixed expression on his face. Other residents sat in upholstered armchairs, arranged as if for conversation, but no one was talking. They seemed to be waiting, but I didn't know what for. I noticed several men and women slowly making their way to and from a bank of locked metal post office boxes. From somewhere beyond the mailboxes, I heard a woman with an angry edge to her voice addressing a younger woman accompanying her. The younger woman—most likely an aide—spoke softly with an African accent in calming tones.

"I don't belong here." But I also wondered, "Is this is my future?"

I had applied for this position of chaplain, which I planned to balance with my work as minister of a small church. Between the two, I would have sort of a full-time job. At the time, I had just turned 62, no one's definition of young. My image of myself, however, was quite different from what I encountered in this senior community. As I was later to discover, this is not unusual. Many residents revealed feeling startled at finding themselves among "all these old people."

My interview for this position had not gone well. I was questioned by three residents representing the committee charged with selecting a chaplain for the community's Unitarian Universalist population. One man on this committee spoke of his wife's descent into dementia, which had occurred over a period of years, and of how difficult that had been for him. He asked what I would say to someone in that position.

I replied that before I said anything, I would listen. I would listen to what was occurring in the lives of those involved and what they thought and felt.

It wasn't the answer this man wanted. "You would *listen*? Wouldn't you talk about the value of life? Wouldn't you encourage that person? Wouldn't you offer assurance that something of worth will come of this?"

"No," I replied, drawing on some thirty-five years in the ministry. "I would listen." Because if there is anything I have learned, it is that you don't walk into a new situation talking, particularly when there are challenges and stress. I first need to know what is occurring through the eyes of those affected. I have also learned that healing itself begins through offering care and respect: listening.

We did not reach a resolution during the interview, and I left feeling that there was no way I would be offered this job. Even if I were, I decided, I should not accept. This was clearly not a good match.

So I was surprised a few hours later to receive a call from the chair of the committee offering me the position. I was even more surprised at my response, which came from deep within: "I would be honored to be your chaplain."

And I have been honored for almost a decade to serve as a chaplain at Riderwood Village, a continuing care retirement community in the Maryland suburbs of Washington, D.C. While my specific responsibilities are to the Unitarian Universalist population, I have considerable contact with other residents in this community of almost 2,500 people. I also enjoy warm and mutually supportive relationships with members of the pastoral ministries staff, who serve a variety of faith traditions.

My initial reluctance and even aversion to what I encountered in the senior center have given way to respect for those I serve and a profound sense of connection. I no longer see age as the defining feature of the residents of this community. Rather, I have come to know them as distinct people and whole individuals. I have also come face to face with my own aging. That first reaction as I entered—"I don't belong here"—was naïve, even arrogant. We are all aging, we're on this journey through life together, we all "belong here."

The shift in my attitude began with conversations. I talked with residents, and they talked with me. There were the initial encounters: "How long have you lived here? Where did you move from? Do you have children? Tell me about them. Do any of them live nearby? How about grandchildren? Great-grandchildren? What kind of work did you do? Do you have hobbies?" Then the conversations went deeper. I heard pieces of life stories: joys, regrets, events that hang on in a person's memory. I heard about accomplishments but also things left unfinished. People asked about me: my family, why I was doing this work, what I was looking for. In the process, we built trust that enabled us to talk easily, make jokes, laugh together—and also face times of challenge. There have been medical emergencies: a fall, a fracture, the discovery of a worrisome lump. There have been losses: family members or friends who die or are no longer able to sustain a relationship, loss of a home, loss of a place in the world, loss of the power to participate fully in the life of a community. And always the relentless hammering of age on our bodies: memory loss, diminished sight and hearing, a knee that hurts all the time, heart problems, a worn-out hip requiring surgery. As one resident put it, "Everybody's got something going on."

I listened to their stories, thoughts and insights, concerns and worries. There were brief chats in hallways, longer talks over a meal or in an apartment, small group conversations. The mantle of strangeness slipped away as we engaged each other at the level of our shared humanity. Now, as I interacted, I saw people who had led long, complex, interesting, productive lives and who had absorbed the lessons of a lifetime. Yes, they were facing challenges, but I also realized: Twenty-five years ago these people ran the world.

As a chaplain, I was called to help. But how? What could I do that mattered? Aging is a condition that cannot be cured, counseled, or prayed out of existence. Despite abundant resources telling of active seniors in full control of their lives, age does catch up with us. We can perhaps slow its advance, take precautions, make sensible choices. But each of us—should we live so long—will encounter the diminishment of powers and faculties that aging brings. Nothing I said or did would change that. How could I contribute to the lives of these people I had come to know and value?

And what about my own aging? As I interact with the residents of this community, I am most likely seeing my future. The odds are that I too will face a period of physical decline. I'll move more slowly, I'll look different, various body parts will break or stop working, physical pain will become a familiar presence in my everyday activities. How will I approach these changes? Who do I want to be in old age?

This book is about meaning and spirit in our later years of aging.

Meaning has to do with what matters to us. What do we care about? What do we commit ourselves to? What moves us and may motivate us to make sacrifices? Viktor Frankl wrote the classic book on meaning, *Man's Search for Meaning,* in which he told of his experiences as a prisoner in several concentration camps during the Nazi era. He noticed that in the conditions of extreme duress of the concentration camps, some prisoners survived and others did not. Some kept on going, no matter what hardships they encountered. Others gave up. He could tell when it was about to happen: a person seemed to stop caring and then died soon afterward.

The primary factor determining whether a person survived was not their physical condition. Frankl notes "the apparent paradox that some prisoners of a less hardy make-up often seemed to survive camp life better than did those of a robust nature." The crucial factor was not the state of one's body but meaning: having something to live for. Those who had something that mattered to them were able to hold on, often tenaciously. Those who didn't gave up.

It's true also in aging. Meaning—having something to live for—makes it more likely that we will bear up to the challenges and indignities that confront us. What does meaning look like as we age? How does what matters to us change, and how does it remain the same?

Spirit reaches into the depths of being and connects us with life's energy. Gerald G. May, Senior Fellow for Contemplative Theology and Psychology at the Shalem Institute for Spiritual Formation, puts it this way in his book *Will and Spirit*: "Spirit has to do with the energy of our lives, the life-force that keeps us active and dynamic." Spirit connects us to the force of existence: the energy that creates, sustains, and renews. The essential spiritual question for a person at any age is "What gives you life?"

As we grow older, we can't do what we once could, but we can still remain engaged; we can stay interested and involved in life. We can appreciate beauty. We can be restored by the fragile scent of a flower, the sharp-sweet taste of an orange, the unself-conscious laughter of a child. We find deep satisfaction when changes in society bring us closer to what we believe is just and right. And we experience disappointment when what we have hoped for and dreamed about is not achieved. We are still sustained by relationships with others, perhaps longtime friends, perhaps new acquaintances. We shed tears of sorrow, tears of joy. We continue to care.

Engagement connects us with life's energy in our later years, even as our level of activity diminishes. What keeps us involved? How may we stay related to the force of life?

All of us are aging all of the time, but in this book I am concerned primarily with the later years. In the senior community where I work, the average age is 85. At this stage, the time ahead shortens. For most of our days, we have decades ahead to anticipate. Now that changes, and long-range plans are for the next generations. What does meaning look like from the perspective of these later years? What gives us life?

This book is also written for those who care for people in their later years. What can we do that helps? What can we do that matters? When I started serving as a chaplain to those in their senior years, I was painfully aware that I did not know what I was doing. But over time—with considerable trial and error—I have learned. While offering such care can be challenging and sometimes exhausting, it mostly involves doing simple things: Showing up. Being present. Listening. Being kind. Being patient. Valuing people. Trusting instincts. I have learned that connecting on a human level matters, even in difficult times. *Especially* in difficult times.

My primary sources for this book are people who have talked with me about their experiences of aging. Some of these were formal interviews; others were informal conversations that took place during the course of ordinary days. Some of the people I talked with were residents of Riderwood Village; others lived in different parts of the country, representing a variety of living situations: in their own homes, living with relatives, in institutional settings.

I am not a journalist, and I am not a researcher. That became clear to me as I engaged in these conversations. I am a minister; my instincts are to support and value. To those of other disciplines, my methods might seem haphazard. I found people to talk with by starting with those I knew, then those who were recommended by people I knew, then those to whom I was referred by those I had already interviewed. While I sought diversity of religion, race, and region, my final criterion of who to interview was whether they would talk to me. If someone was willing, I would listen.

What I looked for in these conversations—and as I have put this book together—was not the facts and figures of aging. Rather, I have been seeking a story. Or, more accurately, stories. We find and create meaning by telling stories through which we give form to the events of our lives. I wanted to know how people conceive of their lives as those lives approach an end. The hope that draws me is that these individual stories come together to form a shared narrative that helps illuminate the conditions we face in our later years. I also hope that these stories might stimulate memories and other stories among those who read this book and in those who participate in discussions generated by the themes I have identified.

The age range of those I interviewed extended from the mid-60s to the mid-90s, with most in their 80s. In citing the ages of those I quoted, I used their age at the time of my interview or my contact with them. In some cases, I have changed names and altered details to protect the privacy of interviewees. I have also edited quotations to account for the differences between spoken language and the written word. In cases where I have made these edits, I have checked with those I was quoting to make sure I correctly interpreted what they were saying.

My own journey also informs this book. When I interviewed for the chaplaincy position at Riderwood Village, I thought I was just looking for a job. But as I have participated in the life of this community, I have found myself drawn in, personally engaged, and immeasurably enriched. I look to these seniors for guidance and wisdom about facing challenges and opportunities presented by aging. As they grow older, some do become frustrated, angry, sad; some withdraw from life. But others stay involved. They remain interested in what takes place in the world and remain in contact with people. In so doing, they offer reassurance about aging: that it is not to be feared, that in our later years there continue to be opportunities for discovery, connection, renewal. They assure me that aging is a natural part of life that can be creatively addressed.

A third source I draw upon is the tradition of contemplative spirituality that finds expression in many faith traditions. At its center is the affirmation that we can draw closer to the force that gives us life. In some traditions that force is named God, while others use different terms to identify the essential energy of being: the Tao, Allah, nature, the light, the ground of being. The contemplative aspires to be present to what is life-giving, renewing, liberating.

We find expressions of contemplative spirituality in most religions, including Christian and Jewish monasticism, Buddhist monks who detach from the things of the world to experience life itself, the Islamic mysticism expressed by the Sufis, and the experiment in simple living at Walden Pond reported by Henry David Thoreau. The process of aging also simplifies, which offers the possibility of experiencing life with greater presence and depth.

In his autobiography, Bertrand Russell—the philosopher, mathematician, and antiwar activist—tells of an occasion that changed him. He and his wife, Alys, shared a summer home with the philosopher Alfred North Whitehead and his wife, Evelyn Wade Whitehead, who suffered from severe angina. One evening, upon returning from a poetry reading, the Russells found Evelyn enduring an acutely painful attack. She seemed cut off from everything and everyone around her.

As he observed his friend with concern and a sense of helplessness, Bertrand Russell found himself transported to what he called "quite another region," in which he encountered the loneliness of each human soul. "Nothing can penetrate it," he thought, "except the highest intensity of the sort of love that religious teachers have preached; whatever does not spring from this motive is harmful, or at best useless."

This encounter with what he called the "core of loneliness in each person" was acutely painful, but it also opened Bertrand Russell to a deeper part of himself, and in the days that followed, he seemed to be in touch with others at a more meaningful level. "I felt that I knew the inmost thoughts of everybody that I met in the street, and though this was, no doubt, a delusion, I did in actual fact find myself in far closer touch than previously with all my friends, and many of my acquaintances."

In the experience of aging, we may encounter that core of loneliness in ourselves and also in others. Each of us is separate; each approaches aging as a distinct being. Yet we share that condition with everybody else: our contemporaries, those who have lived before us, and those yet to come. All of us are alone as we age. In sharing that condition, we are profoundly connected.

The tension between opposites—loneliness and connection, meaninglessness and meaning, diminishment and renewal—produces a creative space from which I draw the energy that drives these reflections.

Aging

*It's different and more difficult than
any of us thought it would be.*
—Barbara L, age 75

Each of us is aging. Always. Day by day, year by year, hour by
hour: Each of us is getting older. Yet when we reach the point
in our lives when we realize, "Oh. Now I am old," it comes as
a surprise. Just about everybody I talk with who is 70 or 80 or
90 expresses a sense of astonishment and disbelief: "How could
this have happened? To *me*? I didn't expect it!" As one woman
put it, with only a slight smile on her face, "I never expected to
be 95, sitting here, talking to you."

Well, after all, we are young for more years than we are old.
When a young person tries to make a point by claiming the
unique perspective of youth, I am tempted to point out, "Yeah,
but I was young a lot longer than you've been young!" One day,
though, we discover that we are not young anymore. It is also
quite common that self-perception lags behind reality; we see
ourselves as younger than we are. A study at the University of

Michigan reported in the *New York Times* found that, on aver-age, people see themselves as thirteen years younger than their chronological age. Many of those I have spoken with cite the experience of looking into the mirror and wondering, "Who *is* that person?" Or of avoiding mirrors because they don't want to see.

But mostly, I think, the sense of disbelief stems from a lack of definition of old age in our society, a lack of guidelines for what it can mean to be old. During most stages of our lives, society gives directions for what we need to do. There are the tasks of childhood: making sense of this world we find our-selves in and learning skills of living. Then we move on to the teenage years, when we seek to define ourselves and how we will relate to the wider community. There are the stages involv-ing school, preparation for a career, perhaps marriage and chil-dren, finding work, accumulating resources, determining what we believe and what we will stand for, seeking ways to contrib-ute to society.

When we approach old age, though, our tasks in life and our roles become more ambiguous. Several people I've talked with have observed that when they were younger, they knew what they were supposed to do and what came next. But now that they are old, the course their life should follow is no longer so clear. Marie G, who is 88, observed, "For most women, if you have a home and a family and a husband, you're focused on that and the welfare of everyone. And that takes precedence over other things. It's not that you don't have other things in your life, but your main emphasis is on your family and what they're doing." But then, she said, it was a "rude awakening" when her husband died and her children established their own homes, their own families. "I really had not ever thought beyond Jack's death—what would happen after that." Or as another woman expressed it, "I don't know how to be old."

There are exceptions. An African-American woman I interviewed reminded me that in African-American culture, the grandmother often plays an honored role in a family, and sometimes raises the grandchildren. "I was raised by my grandmother," she said. And in Asian culture, those who have made it this far in life accrue honor with their age, and younger generations seek their wisdom.

But this is not true in mainstream American culture, which directs its attention toward the young. I recently received a summons for jury duty, so I witnessed the formation of a jury. There was a large pool of people to draw from, and I was interested to see who got the nod—who would be regarded as having sufficient wisdom to render a judgment that would be fair and true. The jury that the court selected was diverse: women and men were about equally represented, people of color outnumbered white people, there were people of different ethnic heritages. This jury was a good microcosm of the community in which I live. Except for one omission: everybody on that jury was young to middle-aged. The oldest person on that jury must have been in his late 30s. There were plenty of older people to choose from, but they were not picked. I wonder why.

A 30-year-old social worker who has chosen geriatrics as her specialty reported that her contemporaries have a hard time understanding why she would devote herself to people in their final stages of life. "They say, 'Oh my gosh. I could never do *that!*' People are in awe, and I think it's because it's a part of the world or our culture that's invisible. And I've always had a strong ethical sense of making visible the invisible." Old people make us uncomfortable, so we keep them out of view. If we don't see them, we might stave off the recognition that each of us is subject to the constraints of age. If we don't encounter old people, perhaps we won't be reminded of our own mortality.

Nevertheless, aging is a rising trend. Medical science keeps finding ways to prolong our lives. Plus, the baby boomers—and the demographic bulge they represent—are poised on the cusp of old age. As a boomer myself, I am accustomed to expecting that the world will pay attention to me and my cohorts, simply because there are so many of us. When we hit old age, we will continue to demand the spotlight.

Several older seniors I talked with observed that much of the material they receive about aging is aimed at younger retirees. There are accounts of trips taken, new interests pursued, businesses started, skills developed, missions to achieve. There are the "bucket lists" to be created and resolutely pursued. A retirement community advertises "the feeling of a perpetual party!" Another ad features an old man crowing, "I'm not a senior! I'm an adventurer!" And, of course, there is the massive coverage of celebrities. We follow their aging—as we do their other stages of life—with breathless fascination. One publication announces that Cyndi Lauper is "still having fun!" Warren Beatty "proves it's never too late!" And Lynda Carter "gets her kicks rowing, cycling—and singing on open water!"

Much of what is available on aging conveys this message: "You can do everything you used to do—and *more*!" Which is lovely, except that it's not true. As we age, we will encounter limitations. Things we once took for granted are no longer possible.

Kate L, who is 87, observed, "A lot of the books that are written are about always feeling good, how to feel better. I'd like to hear some *truth*: the terror and the fear and what's it about." "I tell you," she said, "I was a golden girl. Then I tarnished. Now I'm copper. Old age is not golden. The 'golden years.' What a crock! It's never golden. It's tarnished."

I asked people I interviewed, "How has aging affected you?" JoWynn J, who is 78, put it this way:

> I feel and see the difference in my body and in my mind. I'm slowing down. I no longer run up four flights of stairs. I take the elevator if it's more than two flights of stairs. And I hold on carefully when I walk downstairs. I'm slower and I'm more careful about my mobility.
>
> Mentally, it's harder to find the word I want. Word finding is the first thing that goes—especially now, you know, you can't remember names. And I think my word processing is slower; at least, sometimes it is. I use hearing aids because I have hearing loss. And even with the hearing aids, I sometimes have difficulty following conversations, understanding what people are saying to me. My body shape is changing; my shoulders are getting round.
>
> Oh, and I get up to do something—I think I want something in the kitchen and by the time I get there, I can't remember what I wanted. I also have an imbalance disorder, which is another common characteristic as people age.

We lose capabilities we once took for granted. Climbing a flight of stairs. Walking without a cane or a walker. The assurance that if we fall down, we can get up again. Hearing a conversation clearly, going to a movie or the theater and being able to understand what is being said. Seeing well enough to read, to watch a television program, to recognize faces. Writing with a steady hand. Thinking quickly. Remembering what happened yesterday. Keeping track of what needs to happen today and tomorrow. "I write everything down," one woman reported, "so that I don't forget appointments."

A woman who is living with the early stages of Parkinson's disease spoke of its effects on her everyday life. "One of the frustrations is that I have to pay so much attention to my body. I get up at 4:30 or 5:00 a.m. so that I can complete the morning's routine in time to do anything else. Every night I spend at least twenty minutes getting the meds set up for the next day. And then I have to schedule all these doses and plan that I take them at a certain time." Others dealing with different conditions spoke of the same frustration: addressing the needs of their aging bodies takes up an ever greater percentage of the available time. As one woman put it, "It seems that all my husband and I do is go to doctor appointments."

Another woman observed, "I'm very much slower when I do things. It takes me longer, and my energy wears out, goes away quicker." Many people I talked with referred to reduced energy as a primary component in their experience of aging: it takes more effort to complete tasks, and the energy they do have doesn't last as long. Madeleine B, who has a heart condition, spoke of carefully planning just one activity each day that takes her out of the house. If she tries to do more, she pays for it with fatigue lasting for the next several days. And Ward K, who is 88, said,

> The surprise comes from confronting the reality of the lack of energy. Sure, ten years ago, I knew that as I got

older, I wouldn't have quite as much energy. But now suddenly, here I am, and it's like, "Damn! This is really some bad stuff!" It's the lack of energy and the physical limitations. You talk about them, but it's something totally different to experience them.

As we age, we look different from how we are accustomed to seeing ourselves. Barbara L remembered a morning when she experienced a moment of recognition:

> I wore my hair in bangs. I went to brush the hairs away from my face, and I thought, "Well, what's the matter? I can't brush them." I kept flicking my hand, trying to get what I thought were hairs out of the side of my face around my eyes. And then I went and looked, *really looked* in the mirror, and I thought, "Oh my God, they're wrinkles!"
>
> And that was funny on one level; I could find some humor in it. On another level, I wanted to cry.

Another woman articulated what many may feel: "I hate, *hate, hate* looking in the mirror." The two of us were seated at her dining room table. She got up from her chair and led me to an assemblage of photos of her life at different times. She pointed out one of her as a young woman and her husband as a young man, clearly happy in each other's presence. It seemed important to her that I see who she had been in that earlier time. "I really was a very pretty girl," she said. Then, after a pause, "But I don't think it matters. We're all pretty when we're young."

With aging may also come a sense that the rules by which society operates have changed. This recognition can appear in a variety of contexts. The music people listen to doesn't sound like music to you anymore. Humor is different; what people laugh at today doesn't seem funny to you. Similarly, the jokes you tell may bring polite smiles, not the hilarity you think they deserve. Language changes. Word usage that would have surely earned a red mark of disapproval from your high school English teacher now is found in the pages of the *New York Times*. Clothing styles are also different, sometimes dramatically different, from what had been considered in good taste or even acceptable. I have seen several cycles of what is considered the proper fit for men's clothing: from roomy to slim-fitting, back to roomy (with shoulder pads), and then a look that is more trim. Then roomy again, followed by suits so tight-fitting that just a few years earlier they would have been considered several sizes too small. Those who don't consistently update their closets find themselves walking around in clothes that define them as of another era.

The frame of reference changes as one generation follows another. Life looks different to those who grew up in the Depression and World War II, or the prosperity of the 1950s, or the protests and experimentation of the 1960s and 1970s, or the proliferation of computers and digital technology of the 1980s and 1990s, or the attention given to terrorism in the early twenty-first century. And with those different images from our formative years, different "truths" appear self-evident.

Marie G told me, "Someone was asking what I did when I got out of high school. I got out of high school in 1945 when the war was still going on, and there weren't many things open for women at the time, and most of the jobs for women were as a secretary."

"What's a secretary?" her questioner asked, and Marie struggled to find a way to describe this job, which has mostly disappeared from today's offices. "Well, a secretary," she said, "was sort of the office computer, because you had to remember all the things that people now use their computers for."

Values change. What was considered right and proper in one generation shifts to something else entirely for those in generations that follow. Everyday courtesies that once provided structure for our lives now are no longer observed. Meanwhile, other standards of etiquette are established, such as those that apply to email and social networking. Seniors who venture onto that turf may find themselves having to negotiate new standards and expectations that are not explicitly stated. Recently, my wife and I celebrated our wedding anniversary with dinner in a very nice, rather expensive restaurant. It was, for us, an opportunity for conversation while enjoying good food. But we found ourselves surrounded by other diners staring into their phones. With no electronics in hand, we were oddities in that environment.

A woman reported that her husband doesn't watch new television programs because he doesn't understand what's happening on these shows. He can't figure out the plotline, who the characters are, how they relate to each other. And, besides, the actors "mumble." So the two of them watch old television shows such as *Perry Mason*, *M*A*S*H*, and *Hogan's Heroes* in which they know the characters and can follow the stories.

And then there are the everyday indignities—not the result of malicious intent but because those who have done the planning just haven't taken into account the realities faced by older people: the stairs that need to be negotiated, the spaces too tight for a walker, the restaurant that's dark and noisy. Maybe you would like to take a walk, get out into the neighborhood. But when you attempt to cross the street, the lights are sequenced to move traffic rather than meet the requirements of pedestrians, and you can't get across in the time allotted.

As we age we find ourselves in spaces that were once familiar but now, it seems, have been altered. An 88-year-old man expressed what he felt in a short, poignant statement: "I just don't fit."

ONE

Loss

Things drop out of your life.
—Ethel T, age 88

"Aging is about loss," says Marguerite R, an 83-year-old woman of Greek ancestry. Her short-cut hair is wavy, white with black highlights; she dates memories by its color: "My hair was still black when that happened." She speaks distinctly, smiles frequently, often refers to current events, which she follows by watching cable news broadcasts. When I phone her, I hear the news in the background. When I visit her in her apartment, she turns off the TV so that we can talk.

The police had visited earlier that day. A routine check of a pawn shop turned up a class ring from a Washington, D.C., high school with her initials engraved in it. The police contacted officials at the school, who put them in touch with Marguerite. She hadn't realized the ring was missing but was able to identify several other pieces of jewelry that had also been taken from her apartment.

Marguerite expressed gratitude at recovering these items, some of which were cherished keepsakes. She told the police how impressed she was with their work, reuniting her with goods she hadn't even known were gone. But the experience has left her shaken, feeling vulnerable—she has lost the sense of security that she had taken for granted most of her life.

She grew up in Washington, D.C., and attended public schools in a city that was, at the time, deeply segregated. Children were divided into white and black, each attending separate schools. And the habit of segregation did not stop with that initial division. In the "white" school Marguerite attended, children of certain ancestries found themselves the objects of prejudice. These included Italians, Jews, Poles, and Greeks, like Marguerite's family. This experience of being discriminated against and ridiculed because of her ethnicity helped forge her lifelong commitment to justice; she pledged to protect those who were targets of abuse.

She dreamed of attending law school, which would lead to a career as an attorney. But that path was difficult for a woman to pursue during the era when she was young. Besides, she says, she felt protective of her mother after the death of Marguerite's father. Attending college and graduate school would have compromised her ability to help out. (Later, she realized that her mother was quite capable of taking care of herself and didn't need Marguerite to watch out for her. But Marguerite didn't know that at the time.) So she enrolled in secretarial school to develop skills that would lead to a job.

Her desire to be involved in work for justice found a new avenue of expression. She took a position as a secretary in a law office, thus becoming involved in the cases of clients represented by the firm. She also married the firm's senior partner, leading to a long, happy, and satisfying marriage.

Marguerite tells about the losses she has experienced throughout her life. Most notably, the deaths of her husband, brother, and son—all within a year of each other. More recently, a niece committed suicide. She was in her 20s, "such a beautiful young woman." Marguerite wonders how a person "with so much potential" could feel such deep despair that she would choose not to live. Thinking about how life must have felt to her niece, she says, makes her very sad.

She has also lost friends whom she had known for decades and who recently died. "Losing friends," she says, "is like losing a part of yourself."

There have been other losses as Marguerite has grown older. She walks with a limp; distances once covered in minutes now take much longer and involve frequent pauses to rest. She moves slowly, carefully. Several times she has fallen and been unable to get up on her own and so has had to push the "help" button she wears around her neck. There have been hospital stays to heal from the bruises, the all-over achiness that resulted. She feels grateful that she has not broken bones in her falls.

Marguerite's physical instability has led to a loss of independence. For fifty-three years, she lived in a house in Washington, D.C. "I was the matriarch of the neighborhood," she says with a warm smile at the memory, and she tells of the joy she experienced in the vitality of the city, the people of different backgrounds, nationalities, ages, and races who enriched her everyday life. But the house had stairs, and they were becoming difficult to negotiate. And then there was a very cold and snowy winter, followed by a hot Washington summer. When the weather was hot or cold or icy, she did not leave the house and began to feel like "a prisoner," trapped within. This led to her decision to move to a retirement community where there are no stairs to climb, no need to go outside if the weather is inhospitable, where there is medical care onsite and a community of people to ease her isolation.

She has no doubt, she says, that this was the right time to move and the right place to move to, even though it was so difficult to leave her home and reduce her possessions to what would fit into her new apartment. It meant leaving much behind that had been important to her. Not only were there objects that represented her life, there were also relationships that she had to let go of, including with her neighbors, some of whom had been longtime friends. Especially difficult was the loss of her church, where she had been a founding member. The retirement community to which she moved is a half-hour's drive from her church; she had sold her car and so getting there on a regular basis was not feasible.

And yet, Marguerite remains involved in life. At her retirement community, she has joined the committee that welcomes new residents and orients them to the environment. "I know what it's like," she says. She knows how disorienting the transition can be. Mostly, she reassures people: "You will adjust; you will be OK. After a year, after experiencing all the seasons in this new place, all the holidays, this community will feel like home." Marguerite has joined a congregation at the retirement community, which has eased the loss of her church. She has made new friends, participates in programs, follows current events assiduously, and continues her involvement in work for justice. When a referendum on marriage equality was placed on the Maryland ballot, she was an active advocate, urging residents to vote in favor.

Marguerite sometimes aches at the losses she has experienced; they are real and remain with her. Yet she speaks of being inspired by other seniors she encounters, by their courage as they face disability, as they lose strands of what had constituted the fabric of their lives. It takes courage to face a new day, no matter what our stage in life. But the need for courage increases as we age: courage to participate in life as everyday tasks become more daunting. Marguerite says that she hadn't thought much about courage in her younger years. Now she does, and finds her life enhanced by the examples set by others: "Every day. I mean, you see people struggling like the devil to get on the bus to go on some special trip. They're looking for a little lightness and joy in their lives, and it's not easy. It's not easy for them to make the trip. And I'm observing and learning and trying to face it realistically."

To remind herself of how she wants to live, Marguerite reaches back into her Greek heritage to a novel written by Nikos Kazantzakis: *Zorba the Greek*. Despite the setbacks he encounters and the pain he experiences, Zorba embraces life. He becomes fully involved in whatever presents itself, finding joy in the simplest of activities. "The hardest things are the losses," Marguerite says, "but it's just inevitable. I go back to Zorba: 'Let's dance!' Yes, he died, but 'Let's dance!'" This is what Marguerite aspires to: finding joy in what her life offers at every stage. Becoming involved in whatever presents itself: the good, the bad, and the sometimes tedious every day.

Two years later. Now Marguerite has pulled back from her earlier involvements. She has had more health problems. First her mobility was affected; now she has difficulty expressing herself. This highly articulate woman struggles to find the right words. Her energy is also diminished. A simple errand, attending an activity, interacting with other people—pursuits that once added to the pleasures of a day now require more effort than she can muster. So she stays in her apartment, shrinking her contacts to family and a few close friends. "I know I can call and unload on them," she says.

She approaches these changes with characteristic realism. She reports, "There's a growing patience with all of it. This is the way it is, and this is the price I'm paying for having had 85 years on the planet." And still, she finds gifts scattered throughout her days, ordinary things that delight her. "I very much enjoy just 'the rattling of the blinds.' My daughter says that I must have been a cheap date because there's so much here that I do enjoy."

Looking back at her life, she hopes to leave something behind that influences the next generations. Being Greek is part of that legacy. "And that embraces a huge sense of comedy. A huge sense of tragedy. Being able to express your feelings freely." Furthermore, "Humor is a big part of it. Being able to survive and laugh with people even when bad things are happening." As she reflects upon her life, she realizes, "How rich my life has been. There have been hard things—losing my son was very difficult. Very difficult. But there have been lots of blessings."

Ultimately, she says, "I hope that all my beloved people understand how much I love them."

Loss is part of life at every stage. As children, we lose baby teeth. We lose toys. We lose games. Pets die. Friendships end. As teens, we enter a world of dramatic highs and lows. We try on roles, then cast them off as we search for the person we are meant to be. Losses and gains intertwine, sometimes without our knowing which is which. Throughout adulthood, we are subject to further losses. We lose a job. A dream does not find expression and seems lost. A career path gets blocked. A marriage does not work out as we had hoped. We lose illusions about others and about ourselves. We lose certitude about right and wrong as life's complexities reveal themselves.

Throughout most phases of life, loss has the potential to create possibilities. A chapter ends; a new one begins. A relationship ends; we become open to a new start with a different partner. A job ends, a project fails, our professional life seems to reach a dead end; we seek another realm of endeavor that may be better suited for who we are or for the tenor of the times. Even tragic losses—an untimely death, a disabling illness, whether our own or a loved one's—may reorient us, bring us to realize what we truly value and offer opportunities to act upon these realizations. The losses we experience help us become who we will be.

As we grow older, the losses escalate. There are still opportunities for change and renewal; I am inspired and humbled by those who react to the losses of aging with courage and creativity. But in our senior years there are more and deeper losses to navigate. We leave the world of work that has occupied us throughout adulthood. For much of our lives, we might have defined ourselves by what we did. Now that we're retired, who are we? The children have grown up, and they have their own children and lives of their own that do not revolve around us. A spouse dies, as do friends who have been companions throughout life, and our circle of acquaintances shrinks. We might outlive one or more of our children, which shatters assumptions about the proper course of life through the generations.

Our circle of friends and acquaintances shrinks as they become less able to maintain relationships, as they become sick and die. "The hardest part for me," Barbara P observed, "is that people die all the time. Yeah, that's really tough. I have a bridge partner now who's going to get an EKG today and I told her *she can't die*. None of this; no dying. It's not allowed!" She paused and said softly, "That's the hardest part."

There can be a loss of independence, the ability to be in control of our own lives. Perhaps we are no longer able to live on our own. We have to depend upon others to provide basic services like shopping, cooking, keeping our living quarters clean, transportation. We might reach a time when we can no longer drive. Most of us remember the liberation we felt when we first got a driver's license; it's an important rite of passage in growing up. At the other end of life, when we surrender our license, it's another passage, this time announcing that we are no longer full participants in the adult world.

We also lose physical capabilities: the ability to walk unaided, to hear well enough to follow a conversation, to breathe without effort, to remember names and places, to go through a day without pain, to stand up straight, to be refreshed by sleep. I visited a woman in her 90s whose body was shrunken, and her hands were misshapen due to advanced arthritis. "I'm not sick," she said—speaking from her bed, for her aides had not yet gotten her up that day—"but I'm not well either." No, she wasn't sick; she was old. Her body was weakening, shrinking, shriveling, as happens naturally as the years accumulate.

Medical treatments address many of the physical challenges of aging. They slow the inevitable, offer the possibility of living longer with a better quality of life in the time that we have. But often neglected is the question of meaning—what matters to us. For most people I have met, simply living longer isn't enough. While younger generations celebrate those who hit the century mark, the centenarians, themselves, might not be so pleased about their achievement. As one woman who was confined to her bed said to me, "Just living longer is not necessarily a good thing."

With the loss of people who had been part of our lives, the loss of our professions, the loss of the ability to do what we once enjoyed, there comes also a loss of engagement with others and with the world. We lose interest in the world, in other people, even in ourselves. We don't keep up with what had once engaged us; we don't develop new interests. In the retirement community where I serve, some residents close their doors. They come out of their apartments mainly to pick up a meal and bring it back inside. They do not participate in the activities of the community. They let friends drop away. They eat alone; the social contact involved in sharing a table with other diners is too daunting.

And so the questions present themselves. Who am I now? How does my life matter? Where can I find meaning? One 90-year-old man expressed a concern shared by many of his contemporaries as he worried, "I'm just taking up space. I'm not contributing anything."

Also, spirit—the life force. As we age, we may find that we have less energy. Perhaps I can undertake only one activity in a day that takes me away from home. I yearn for replenishment: the renewal of spirit that engages me in life. It used to come more easily. Now, how do I recover the spirit that keeps me in relationship with other people, in relationship with the world around me?

A woman spoke of her mother, who had reached a stage of life when she was withdrawing from everything and everyone:

My mom is 98, and until 97, she was still a pleasant person. She made friends, and she would go get dressed and have lunch, and she still read the paper. Into her 90s, she took a course every semester in current events at the local college.

Then she fell two years ago and just has gone downhill, and now she doesn't do anything. She doesn't read. She doesn't watch television. She doesn't want to talk very much. I think she's deeply depressed and medicated. She pretty much just stares and complains. When she does speak, it's to complain and, of course, she has reasons to complain. She'll get emotional and say, "I don't know why I'm alive. Every morning, I wake up, I open my eyes, and I'm so sorry that I'm awake." It's heartbreaking.

In her professional life, Ellen C had a career in business, with an MBA from the Wharton School and a position doing economic analysis of major capital spending projects for a large freight railroad. She devoted considerable time and effort as a volunteer, initiating a capital campaign for her church and shepherding it through to a successful conclusion. She also established a program aimed at funding projects in congregations throughout the region. Thirty years later, she said, this program has distributed over $2.25 million to support new ideas and possibilities in churches.

After retiring, Ellen and her husband joined the Peace Corps, where she taught corporate finance to CPA students in Kenya. Then, after completing her term as a volunteer, she joined the Peace Corps staff and become an overseas administrative officer, first in Kyrgyzstan and then in the Ukraine.

Even after retiring from the Peace Corps, she continued to consult, troubleshooting problems that occurred in different areas throughout the world. "It was," she said, "a job I loved."

When she returned home, Ellen again became active in her church, directing her attention to the finances of both her local congregation and the regional organization. Then she and her husband moved to a retirement community in a different state, where she joined a nearby church and again helped address its financial and organizational needs. "I'm glad when I can bring some order out of chaos," she said.

Ellen likes to "make things happen." In her retirement community, she came up with the idea for the chaplaincy position that I now hold, and she promoted it. When some in that community were skeptical about its viability, she figured out what needed to be done to convert the idea into a workable program and then spearheaded efforts to bring it from concept to reality. She said, "It is one of the projects I am proudest of."

So, yes, Ellen likes to make things happen. This has been an important source of meaning throughout her life. Today, though, she feels frustrated. As she grows older, she has found it more difficult to be involved in efforts that bring change. She retains her ability to evaluate challenges to an organization and develop means of addressing them, but her opportunities for making a difference have diminished.

When she and her husband moved to another part of the country to be closer to family, it was difficult to find a place for herself in a new church. The people in congregations she visited seemed interested in different things than she was. Also, there weren't opportunities for her to become involved, especially given the physical difficulty of just getting to church. She still drives but not at night. Committee meetings are usually held in the evening and so that reduces her opportunities for involvement. She told me,

> I'm not active in church anymore—whereas in the past, I've done all I could do. Now I go to church maybe once a month, and then I go home.
>
> Once you can't drive or don't want to drive, it's just a lot nicer to stay at home. You're not going to be on the board, you're not going to be on the social action committee, you're not going to do anything. And so why not just stay home? And especially for me, the service is no longer inspiring. So what's the point?
>
> Now I play bridge a lot, I go to board meetings at the retirement community, I'm in the book club, but I'm not *changing* anything.

That's a loss. When what used to bring meaning to your life becomes less viable, it creates a sense of emptiness. There is space where once there was activity, engagement, opportunity. What do we do with that open space? Does it get filled with another activity or another realm of interest—or not?

When others stop valuing what we have to offer, and when opportunities to contribute to other people's lives dry up, that too is a loss. There comes a point, as we age, when much of the world stops listening to what we have to say. This may have little to do with the value of our contributions, their relevance, or their perceptiveness. Rather, it's about age. When we are perceived as old, people don't pay attention to us as much as they once did—even those who love us. I had a conversation with two men over lunch in their retirement community. Both had had distinguished professional careers, both remained acute observers of local activities and the national scene. They noted, with some bitterness, their sense that even though the residents of their community bring with them expertise, competence, and life experience, their input is sought only to a limited degree. On crucial matters, the thoughts and suggestions of residents might even be considered a distraction, hindering the efficient functioning of the organization.

This is a theme I often encountered among those who are in their 80s and 90s. They find themselves in a world now run by younger people who don't value what older people have to contribute. And while these seniors may "understand" that the next generations deserve their turn, they still feel left out. There is a disconnect between what older people feel they have to offer and what younger people are willing to accept. "So yeah," one 88-year-old man put it, "I feel like a bit of a ghost."

"We're seeing a lot more mental illness: anxiety disorders, personality disorders. I'm not sure where that's coming from," observed a social worker who specializes in serving the elderly. When I asked about the key challenges she faces in her work with seniors, she responded, simply, "Dementia. I mean, one word: that's it. There are different types of dementia and cognitive impairment, but that's really the main problem."

That observation correlates with my work among seniors. The greatest fear that I encounter—even more than death—is the loss of mental functioning: the ability to remember, to reason, to follow a line of thought, to carry on a meaningful conversation with another person, to make plans, to arrive at an appointment on time, to complete a simple task.

There is a complicated interaction between physical changes in our bodies that bring on such symptoms and the choices we make that may either minimize or intensify these changes—between effects of our aging that are due to conditions over which we have little control and the power we all have to influence how our aging will proceed.

Physical changes come to us no matter what steps we take to delay their advance. Our bodies are mortal and will ultimately break down. Our minds, as part of our bodies, share that fate. In general, the longer we live, the more likely we are to experience some diminishment of mental functioning. And our bodies age at different rates. Some people are exhausted by the time they reach their 60s or 70s. Others remain vital and active well into their 90s.

But another contributing factor is the lack of opportunity to make a difference. When the expertise we have developed throughout our lives is no longer sought or valued—perhaps no longer even relevant—we lose sources of meaning that have guided us as well as opportunities for connection with each other and with the wider community. When we lose a sense of our place in the world, then our own power to participate and contribute diminishes.

And then people begin to choose to refrain from participating. This may be a response to physical changes; it may come from a sense that others no longer value what we have to offer; it may be due to a certain weariness that can come from having "seen it all," "done it all." Any and all of these factors can contribute to a decline in our mental functioning. I see people withdraw from participation and then begin a spiral of decline. Muscles weaken through lack of exercise—any muscles, whether physical or mental. They weaken and finally atrophy if they don't get used.

Further complicating this picture is our natural tendency toward denial. Sometimes we refuse to notice or accept changes that have occurred in our powers and abilities. There is the man who resists surrendering his driver's license when anyone who has observed his unsteady hand on the wheel can see in a moment that he presents a hazard to himself and others who share the road. There is the woman who holds tightly to the reins of her business and delays turning it over to the next generation because, in her opinion, only she knows the proper way to run it. There are those who insist on participating in activities in which they can no longer keep up.

Ellen C cited the example of the groups in which she plays bridge:

> I'm in three bridge clubs, believe it or not, and they're all different. The Monday one is the hardest to play in because there are so many people who have lost it. But you play with them anyway because they need it; it's their only social life. And so we all do it, even though it's very hard to play in that group.
>
> One woman is 97 and just quit doing her own taxes; I can't imagine what the poor IRS guy had to read. But, you know, people come, and they want to play bridge, so you play with them. There's another guy who has dementia, but he was a mathematician, and he can still keep score. Amazing. You just try to support those people as best you can.
>
> There was another woman; she had to go into assisted living. She had been such a good bridge player, but she went downhill. The last time I played with her, she took four cards out of her hand and put them down like they were a trick. Well, you can't do that. It took me five minutes to convince her to put them back in

her hand and play them. And she didn't understand.
We told the nurses not to bring her anymore—I mean,
if you can't even play your cards. And she told somebody very sadly that she was asked not to come. She's
blaming it on us that we don't ask her. The truth of the
matter is that she can't play.

My grandfather was a highly skilled cabinetmaker who
built furniture of startling complexity and beauty. In his
later years, my father brought him a small project: to make a
wooden frame on which to mount a commemorative plaque. I
remember how pleased my grandfather was to receive this task.
He even did a little bragging about how he had been entrusted
with it.

I also remember the product he handed over to my father. It
was a mess. The surface of the wood was rough with several visible
chunks, the angles were not square, the finish had been unevenly
applied. My grandfather handed it over to my father without
apology, as a finished piece. My father thanked him, quietly put
it away, and then purchased what he needed at a variety store. It
seemed that my grandfather had not noticed the inferior quality
of the piece he delivered. How could he not see that?

All this is loss. Loss of opportunities to use skills we have
spent a lifetime developing. Loss of our ability to contribute
to the life of a community as we once did. Loss of our power
to participate, to influence other people, to make things or
change things or imagine possibilities. Loss of physical capacities and mental powers that we once took for granted. Loss of
our capacity to even recognize when we are no longer able to
function at the level we previously did.

In her professional life, Evelyn N was a high school teacher. A native of a small town in Iowa, she moved to the East Coast as a young married woman. "I had always wanted to live in the East," she told me. "And I did it!" Her husband provided that opportunity when a position opened for him in Washington, D.C. They raised their two children, and she taught in the local schools while enjoying the museums, galleries, and concerts that were now available to her.

Today, Evelyn is quite healthy, physically, for a woman of 85 years. The only medications she takes are over-the-counter. Her primary problem is significant short-term memory loss. She doesn't remember appointments; she sometimes gets lost in the halls. In a conversation, she will often repeat the same question or the same statement several times within minutes. But she recognizes people, she remembers some events. She has a record of falling but thus far has shown a remarkable ability to fall without seriously injuring herself. Yet some of these falls occurred in her apartment, and she was not able to get up on her own, so she waited until she was discovered.

After one such fall, she was hospitalized. Upon her return, she remembered having been in the hospital—and that she didn't like it—but she couldn't say why she had been there. "Evelyn, why were you in the hospital?" I asked. "I haven't the foggiest idea," she replied. Then she offered a theory: "Maybe it was an infection."

She now lives in an apartment in the assisted living section of her residence community. She doesn't like living there. It's too far away from her friends, from being able to do simple things like meet them for dinner. She has a close friend with whom she sometimes goes to dinner, and she looks forward to those occasions. Yet her friend is getting worn out, both by the physical effort of getting there and by the worry that comes from needing to be aware of her constantly. There is always the risk that Evelyn will wander away and get lost.

One of Evelyn's friends tells me about the strain of ordering a meal. Evelyn declines ordering until others at the table have finished. Then she'll say, "I'll have what she's having." She doesn't understand the menu well enough to place her own order.

Evelyn says to me, "Oh, I suppose I am doing fine. The people treat me well. But I don't like it here." She tells me that she's bored, that she's lonely, that she gets so frustrated by not being able to do things she wants to do. When she pauses, I comment, "It feels good to say that, doesn't it?" She nods and flashes the first smile I see from her that day. "Yeah. It feels good."

Where is meaning for Evelyn? And where is there life?

Barbara M said that her greatest loss was the sickness and death of her husband; they had been married for twenty-six years when he died. She said that the term *diminishment* resonated with her. "Diminishment is precisely what I feel. My Great Work has been accomplished. I don't believe I will ever be able to undertake such an all-encompassing emotional and spiritual task again."

The "Great Work" she referred to was taking care of her husband, John, during the year of his final illness. Those responsibilities were especially demanding for her, since he chose a course of treatment using alternative medicine and did not seek more conventional care.

In the decade prior to his getting sick, Barbara said, he had only two checkups with a physician. He did see a chiropractor regularly because of a bad back, and he took many vitamins as well as other supplements. But when his back pain became worse and then was accompanied by a recurring fever, John agreed to a blood screening, which showed extremely high PSA levels, an indicator of prostate cancer. He refused a referral to a urologist and would not consider standard medical treatments.

Instead, he followed a naturopathic regimen featuring supplements and close attention to his diet. Barbara set aside her other responsibilities and focused her attention on him. She made the meals prescribed for naturopathic healing; she attended to his care as he grew weaker, requiring a wheelchair and administration of oxygen.

Caring for her husband was stressful and demanded her full attention and energy, particularly since he was reluctant to have others visit or call. "He just couldn't stand to see the expression on someone's face when they saw how sick he was," she said. As a result, Barbara became his sole caregiver. "I had to be on with maximum power all the time," she said. Yet she reported that it was also a rich experience, as she and her husband found their relationship deepening throughout that year. There was "lots of talking about everything we had enjoyed and being in our own sacred space in the home we created." She would take John outside, push him in a wheelchair, find a shady spot in their yard or in a little park down the street from their home. Then she would return to the house to get the oxygen tank and bring it out to him. "We would just read for a couple of hours, watching people go by, kids, dogs. There was nothing else we had to do. That was really the focus of our last months—just being together."

Halfway through that year, John agreed to bring in hospice, which helped both of them. He loved and trusted the nurse who came to call each week, while Barbara was grateful for the support and advice the nurse brought. She was also someone Barbara could call if confronted with a situation she did not know how to address. Her own isolation eased.

She shared a memory from that year that made her smile:

> This is a cute story. The chair of our church's caring committee is a nurse, and so she came over once—she just wanted to bring something. She brought two little Bundt cakes. John had never liked desserts, but that looked really good to him. So he ate one immediately while she was sitting there. It turns out that people dying of cancer often have cravings for sweets. Then John and I had to drive to the Bundt place at least once a week and get five or six of them. She just completely by chance brought something that he turned out to enjoy tremendously.

After John died, Barbara was left to adjust to the loss of her primary companion. This opened a vast space in her life, which had been consumed with caring for him. Where there had been intensity, now there was openness, silence. "When I was taking care of John," she remembered, "it was electric." She had to be attentive all the time. But then, "afterwards, it was so empty."

For the first several months after her husband died, Barbara continued to feel the residue of stress, hypervigilance, and anxiety that had built up. She spent time with her family, took walks, gardened, attended a yoga class—all activities that helped relieve the tension that she had lived with for the previous year. Then, as she gradually became calmer, "the real sadness just poured in."

Over time, those feelings too become less intense. The sadness didn't go away, but a sense of peace and acceptance began to grow within her. Where loss had been paramount, she now found herself becoming quieter, more thoughtful. The emptiness itself began to feel comforting.

> I did a lot of cleaning, clearing away things. And that was helpful. As the stress gradually eased, this sense of calmness stayed.
>
> It took real effort to be with other people again. So I went to church on Sundays, a little at a time. I met old friends—all people who were very comfortable to be with, people who don't ask a lot of intrusive questions, people I trust.

She also used this time to clean and empty and reorganize the home that she had shared with her husband. He had been an Internet programmer and accumulated a great deal of equipment and resources related to the ever-changing nature of his trade. Barbara found herself "taking carloads of computers and cables and all kinds of devices and attachments to the recycling center and emptied out a couple of file cabinets of old computer magazines, and I've been through the garage. It gave me something to do that was constructive and a place to put my energy. It also helped me feel more peaceful in this space."

Clearing out the closets also brought a sense of direction and purpose to her days. Barbara donated some of John's clothes to charity, while family members took other pieces. "My stepsons wear John's clothes all the time. That makes me so happy! It's a kind of visual reflection of how they are integrating him into their daily reality."

She reported,

I talk to John's pictures. Some of the older women at church have told me in confidence that they do the same thing. I kind of tread carefully on those subjects, but it turns out that a lot of people have a sense of connection with a spouse that is so strong and so deep. I have dreams; I see John out of the corner of my eye. I feel his presence and that could be his spirit—it could be my unconscious. Any and all of those possibilities— it doesn't really matter to me.

Our losses stay with us, particularly those that are the deepest. Gail T, who is 76, served as a financial advisor with a special focus on widows after her own husband died. The women she worked with sometimes asked, "When does it stop hurting?" The only answer she could give was "It may never. But it will not be as intrusive as it is now. You will always have those memories if you wish to call them up, but after a while, you will have the option to call them up or not."

For Barbara M, her loss introduced her to new activities, forced her to develop new skills, initiated her into new experiences. She realized, "I can't go back and have the life I did have, but there are still things that are really beautiful and meaningful and worth doing." For example, "I cut down a tree myself, a tree that had frozen the previous winter—I'd never used a chain saw. I had stacked wood, but to do the whole thing—that was a milestone. I've done some plumbing and electrical work. I had to get a new printer. I'm a totally nontechnical person but I opened the directions, and I did it myself!"

Beyond the new experiences she encountered and the skills she developed, Barbara found a deepening of her spirituality:

I'm in a different emotional space than I've ever experienced. I'm observing and analyzing, and as I move through it, I'm watching and seeing how things shift, as I try to understand the meaning of this chapter I'm in.

A quieter time to reflect and integrate these immense life experiences is really all that I ask.

Barbara L observed, "If there is such a thing as successful aging—and I'm not sure there is—it's really dependent on how a person handles loss."

Aging is about loss. Our lives change, and we can't bring back what has been; we can't return to who we once were. We can influence some of these losses. We can forestall physical changes by attending to our health and by remaining active. We can counteract the diminishment of our place in the world by developing new interests and participating in organizations more in accord with what we have to contribute. We can read and write and do crossword puzzles to keep mentally sharp. We can resist the isolation that comes with aging by entering into new relationships and participating in a variety of communities.

But losses will still occur. They are part of the normal flow of existence. And so the challenge of aging is less about resisting or denying the changes than it is about finding ways to incorporate them into our lives.

This may mean replacing what has been with something new: new activities, new patterns in everyday life, new priorities. For some, a deepening of relationships offers support that helps them negotiate the challenges of this new life they are entering. For some, the losses that aging brings are balanced by a deeper understanding and appreciation of life itself. Elaine

S observed, "As you get older, you lose things, but you gain. Maybe you gain depth, is what I'm saying." And some report their sense that a creative force of existence flows through them, presenting options and offering possibilities, conveying a sense of love and support that holds them as they address the inevitable transitions with which they are confronted.

But always, response to loss involves adaptation: recognizing that conditions have changed and making adjustments. Responding to loss involves addressing change.

I.

What losses have you experienced in your life? How have they affected you?

2.

It is sometimes said, "As one door closes, another opens." Have you experienced this? What opportunities have presented themselves as you have gotten older?

3.

What have you decided to keep and what to leave behind? How have you made these choices?

4.

Is there anything you held on to that you now wish you had let go of? Is there anything you are still holding that you would like to discard?

TWO

Change

You adjust, find another way.
—Mildred H, age 86

I remember how my grandmother changed when my grandfather died. Perhaps she did not see any changes in herself. She might have said that she was still the person she had always been. But I experienced her differently, and our relationship changed.

Herman and Anna were married for sixty years. As a young couple, they had fled Germany with their 3-year-old daughter as war clouds gathered that would grow into the Great War, later renamed World War I. Herman and Anna settled in west central Illinois, and raised a family of five daughters who married and established their own families.

My grandfather was a skilled craftsman who built custom furniture. He started a business, employed other craftsman from Germany whom he sponsored as immigrants. He was a voluble man, interested in far more than his work—philosophy, science, religion, nature study, social policy—and had strong opinions in each realm. He was an amateur actor who appeared in local community theater productions, and he was a public speaker who met regularly with the Toastmasters, an organization that helps participants develop communication and leadership skills. He was a collector of stamps, butterflies, shells, rocks, wood veneers—pretty much anything that caught his interest. He was a stalwart member of his church, directing the children's Sunday school for many years. In that era before specialization shrank the range of activities in which we can profitably engage, he pursued whatever interested him, living intensely, taking advantage of what life offered.

My grandmother made this possible. She functioned quietly and effectively in the background, tending to the children, making do with the family's sometimes fragile finances, ensuring that there was food on the table and clothing for their children, which she often made herself. She provided a foundation that supported my grandfather's more extroverted lifestyle. As he aged, my grandfather became ever more dependent upon her to remember appointments, to dress properly, to make sure he ate, to keep him on track when his attention wandered, to help him leave a social engagement when it was time to go. I have enduring memories of my grandmother gently disengaging him, because he would never leave on his own when there was an opportunity for another conversation.

When Herman died, a void opened in Anna's life. "Now I won't be able to talk with him anymore," she said as we gathered to plan his memorial service. Members of the family wondered how she would bear up, now that the person around whom she had organized her life was no longer with her.

The role that my grandfather had played in her life could never be filled again. And yet I noticed a change in her—a positive one, from my perspective. Whereas she had previously resided largely in his shadow, Anna now stepped into the light. I became acquainted with her as a person in her own right. While she had previously deferred to my grandfather as he told his stories, now she told her own stories: living in Germany as a girl, serving as an *au pair* for a family in France, meeting my grandfather at a social gathering for young people. He was short, she was tall. "*Please* don't let him ask me to dance," she murmured to herself as he made his way toward her.

Anna spoke of the perils involved in their escape from Germany, which had to be kept secret. She remembered how her body went tense when a conductor on a local bus in their town asked, "Where to?" and her 3-year-old daughter announced loudly, "We're going to America!" Thinking quickly, Anna produced a chuckle and said, "Oh, *everybody* wants to go to America," and the danger passed. She talked about the challenges of making a life in this new country, surviving the Depression by growing and canning much of the food that fed her family, the joy she found in being an American. "It was the best decision we ever made," she said, shaking her head in wonder—some sixty years later—at their audacity in leaving everything they had known to start this new life.

After the death of a spouse in a long-term marriage, I have often seen the survivor become more available to others. Aspects of that person that had previously been hidden within the primary relationship now become visible, and we encounter them in their fullness. This, in turn, makes a deeper relationship possible. New life enters to fill the void created by loss.

Throughout our lives, the attitude we take toward life's changes helps determine who we are. As we reach old age and the changes escalate, our ability to respond creatively becomes a primary factor shaping our ability to negotiate the later years.

Faced with the loss of what had been our place in the world—whether in the workplace or as a parent raising a family—do we find ways to move on into this new phase of life, or do we cling to what has been? Faced with the changes in our appearance that aging brings, do we adapt, or do we struggle to maintain the look that had been ours? Faced with the loss of people who had been central to us, do we reach out to form new relationships, or do we hang on to memories of what was? Faced with the decline in our physical capacities, do we withdraw into comfortable spaces, or do we adapt as necessary to stay involved in the activities of our community? Faced with the diminishment of our skills and our stamina, do we find ways to continue learning and developing skills in different realms?

Peggy Z is 85 years old and has been a professional artist all her life. When she was 73, she and her husband downsized. They moved from a big house, which was becoming difficult to maintain, into a much smaller apartment in a retirement community. This move required dismantling and discarding works she had produced and tools of her trade that she had accumulated.

"I had a tremendous studio of everything I made," she said. "I had a drafting table, the work tables, I made them. I made the frames for silkscreen paintings. All that had to be destroyed, knocked down. We had a rental truck that was filled with four thousand pounds of stuff for the trash. That's two tons!"

Once she had finished selling, giving away, and throwing away, Peggy assumed that her days as an artist were over. There wasn't room in her new residence to produce such work. Besides, she was tired from the process of moving out and moving in, and she had a bad back. "I thought that all physical activities were over and I could just lie back."

But she became restless, looked for new avenues of expression. She joined a knitting group that produces items for charity. Then she found herself in charge of putting their projects on display in a public area, climbing a ladder and placing the objects in a tall glass case. Then she set up a yoga studio at the community where she lives, "fighting bureaucracy all the way." A Chinese American, she formed a Chinese music group, scouring the web for recordings and encouraging the members who spoke Mandarin to write out the lyrics of folk songs phonetically so that all could participate. She was also asked to join the Diversity and Inclusion Committee, whose mission is to open avenues of understanding among people of different backgrounds, races, ages, sexual orientations, and economic positions. Peggy observed, "Slowly, I was doing a lot."

She resumed her work as an artist, but in different media. "I went small," she said. That is, she worked in realms that did not require the facilities and the space of her previous pieces. She discovered digital art and created brightly colored prints that seem to pulse with motion. She produced fiber art and also wood constructions. "I found the woodshop [in the retirement community], and I go down there and look for scraps. You'd be surprised what people throw away!" These art forms stretched her in new ways; her work became fresher because she wasn't just repeating themes she had previously explored.

Peggy was asked to mount an exhibit of her art at a local church, which led to several sales and an invitation to curate a show of art produced by seniors, "A Feast for the Eyes." This was a huge undertaking, bigger than anything she had previously worked on. "This project was so different and so big that it could be overwhelming. It involved seniors who have had a lifetime of making good art in great supply and who are not physically able to present it. This is art that would otherwise never have been seen and shared."

Several years earlier, when she had entered the retirement years, Peggy felt worn out, finished as an artist. But now she found, "The more I did, the stronger I got—age or not." The responsibility she felt for the show and the attentiveness to detail it required drove her on. "As a result, at the age of 81, I had produced the biggest and best art show of my career."

That show was repeated annually for four years, each showing completely different art from what had been featured in previous years. "I consider this to be the highlight of my career," she said, "if not my life!" Furthermore, it helped her develop capacities that had lain dormant, surprising her at what she was able to do. "It brought me out of my previous introverted and reserved personality and showed to myself that I can indeed lead and work with more than fifty people. To discover this at 81 is remarkable!"

As a Chinese American, Peggy misses the respect shown in her culture for those who have grown old. American culture is different, she observes; youth is valued, not age. She had absorbed those attitudes herself, assuming that her senior years would be a time in which she would withdraw from the life she had created. So it has been a pleasant surprise to find herself creatively engaged as she makes her way through her 80s. "I think my energy at this age is spurred on by the knowledge that I have done some good things for others."

Bettie Y too has found much that is positive as she has aged. Bettie, who is in her early 70s, speaks of how difficult it was to leave her home and move to smaller quarters. "I had lived in that house over forty years, raised my children there from babies, gone through my whole adult life there. It took me a very long time to adjust that this is my home now. And after three years, I'm still reaching for where things were in the old house."

And yet Bettie considers this to be the best time in her life. Partially, this is because she is involved in activities she finds engaging. Soon after retirement, she became a volunteer in a state legislator's office, which she found to be an exciting environment in which to work. She would still be in that office, except that travel during the winter became challenging. She then became active on the Resident Advisory Council in the community where she lives, which offered opportunities for her to help improve the lives of residents while also forming new relationships herself.

These are also good years for her because she has been able to let go of her old habit of self-criticism, questioning herself, feeling uncertain in new situations. At this stage of her life, she has been able to enjoy who she is. She said,

> For me, the gain in aging has been comfort in my own skin and trust in my judgment.
>
> I have had a lot of jobs in my life, and my last was the best job I ever had. I went to that job at age 54, and I worked there until I was 67, and it was somewhere in that span of time that I just liked who I am, trusted

myself. I've been a pretty insecure person for most of my life, and that went away, and it's nice for it to be gone.

You get to a place, and you're not struggling anymore, and you're not self-doubting. You get to a place where you're just OK. You just have to live to get there.

Elaine S is an 81-year-old for whom staying active is an important goal. But she finds that achieving that aim involves being realistic about what she can and cannot do. When asked what advice she would give for those who are looking ahead to their own aging, she replied, "Live life to the fullest, but recognize who you are." And as we get older, this includes understanding our limitations.

She spoke about an experience that drove this lesson home. She was meeting a friend to see a matinee performance at a theater. Getting there involved taking a subway to her destination. But there were problems on the line she was traveling, her train was emptied, and she stood on the platform waiting for another train. When that train finally came, she boarded it but realized she was going to be late for the performance. She decided, "I can walk faster than this train is going," and so got off, climbed back up to street level, and walked as fast as she could.

When she had just about arrived at the theater, she was exhausted. "My legs gave out from under me, and I fell flat on my face!" She recalled, "A wonderful couple came and helped me up. They took me to Starbucks, and I got something to eat because I hadn't eaten, and they saw me to the theater. I thought afterwards, 'You're not 20, you're not 30, you're not 40; you're 80! You can be late to things.'" She learned that she will need to make allowances in order to continue doing the things she enjoys. She can't proceed with the same intensity as she did when she was younger.

Elaine notes the emphasis on youth in popular culture. "You know, 60 is the new, I don't know, 30 or 40—and it's ridiculous! We're older and I think we should accept it. I don't color my hair. It's sort of silvery now, and I love it when people —young men, especially—open the door for me, or I go with somebody who is younger, and they take my arm. I used to think, 'I can do it alone.' I don't anymore, and I thank them. So, I think that you give up gracefully, but you don't have to give up everything. You just take it at a slower pace or you say, 'Well, I can't do thus and such, but I *can* do this.'"

For Elaine, this attitude of acceptance has been freeing, enabling her to remain engaged with life. Paradoxically, accepting the limitations of aging has made it possible for her to stay active. Rather than resisting or trying to deny the losses, she acknowledges them. Then she considers what she can realistically do, and how to make that happen.

Pat K, who is 73, spoke of her husband's back surgery, which had not gone well. Previously he had been very athletic, but following surgery he became paralyzed. The paralysis eventually receded, but it took a long time. Pat remembers telling her husband, when he was in the rehabilitation center, "You will be able to do whatever you want to do, but you may have to do it differently than you ever thought of before." She applies that insight to the aging process in general. It brings changes to our lives: perhaps in mobility, perhaps in memory, perhaps in independence and the ability to do what we want whenever we want. But given those limitations, we can still have a life—a life with meaning and a sense of possibility—if we make adjustments.

Lowell S, a retired newspaperman in his 70s, spoke of his mother and her sister, how they had faced aging in quite different ways. His mother was able to make adjustments and found meaning and joy in her final years. His aunt was not able to change. Her later years became, to him, a cautionary tale of who he does not want to become as he ages.

His aunt had been a successful businesswoman—a trailblazer, actually—in a time and a business in which there were few women in authority. For her entire career, she worked for a railroad that became part of the CSX system. To rise in the ranks as a woman required considerable strength and self-confidence—her nephew called it "feistiness." For example, when she was passed over for a promotion that went to a less qualified man, she confronted her supervisor—and the next time a comparable position opened, she got it. The same thing happened when she discovered she was being paid less than men at her level. Again she raised the issue; again she got results.

She devoted her life to her work, traveled extensively, held positions of high responsibility, was well paid. She married but did not have children. And when she retired, she settled into her apartment in North Baltimore, where she and her husband had moved when it was first built. But then she got stuck, did not know what to do next. She couldn't adjust to retirement and to the changes that aging brought. If she couldn't participate in life at the level to which she had been accustomed, then she wouldn't participate at all. She became a recluse, rarely venturing out, making no effort to meet other people. After a while, she was the oldest person in the building, rarely seen by the other residents and known by none of them.

She didn't eat well, existed on the nutritional supplement Ensure. Meals on Wheels could have easily delivered food to her, but she refused. "That's charity," she said. "I don't need charity." And in fact she did not need charity; she had plenty of money. But she wouldn't accept any kind of help because of her pride. Eventually she told her nephew Lowell—who told me this story—that she didn't want him to visit her anymore. He refused. "You are my favorite aunt," he said. "I am going to visit you, whether you like it or not." And she didn't like it, because she did not want to be seen the way she was.

Inevitably, there was a fall—more than one. And she couldn't take care of herself anymore. She moved into a nursing home where she yelled at the staff, yelled at the other residents, and refused to cooperate. Having retired from her career, she had lost the meaning that had driven her life and was not able to adjust to this change. Nothing mattered anymore.

By contrast, Lowell cited the example of this woman's sister, Grace, who was Lowell's mother. In her later years, Grace faced escalating health problems, including the loss of her sight, that also put her in a nursing home. But her adjustment followed a different trajectory.

Until she was in her mid-90s Grace lived in her own apartment, where she maintained an active life. But as her eyesight diminished, she was no longer able to live alone safely, and so she moved—under protest—to a nursing facility. At first, she was deeply depressed in that new environment. Lowell would visit and find her in her room, staring out the window (even though she was blind). She wouldn't engage with other people; she barely spoke to him.

A friend came to visit. Grace and Helen had known each other for most of their lives, and Grace did the same routine of staring out the window, barely speaking. This happened during several visits, until Helen lost her patience. She finally said,

"Grace, it's really hard for me to walk over here from where I live." (Helen was 96 at the time.) She continued, "It's difficult but I'm willing to do it because we've been friends all our lives. But if you're going to sit there and ignore me, I'm not coming anymore. I need you to be willing to talk with me." Grace said that the message from her friend came like a lightning bolt, bringing her back to herself.

That moment of recognition coincided with another event. Her doctor recognized that she was depressed and prescribed medication. After some resistance, Grace grudgingly agreed to try an antidepressant, but "only small doses, small pills."

According to Lowell, the difference was nearly immediate. After having been withdrawn and uncommunicative, his mother returned to being "an alert old lady who followed state politics and would talk to anybody. Like night and day." Looking back, Lowell said that it was probably the combination of the intervention of her longtime friend and the medication that made the difference.

Grace's attitude became quite different from the way it had been, quite different from that of her sister: she reached out to other residents of the nursing home, made friends with the staff, became much beloved. Lowell remembered coming to visit her one day and not finding her in her room. He asked a staff person where she was and was directed to a meeting room where a religious service was being conducted. He saw her in the back row, came in quietly, told her he was there. She responded, "Get me out of here!" So he took her outside where there was a small garden. It was a warm day, and Grace had been a gardener all her life. Even though she now couldn't see, she loved sitting amid the flowers of that garden, taking in the sounds and the fragrances and the breezes gently flowing by.

Grace found ways to connect to life, even though the form of these connections was different than it was in her earlier years. She adjusted to the changes that age brought. In so doing, she made this phase of life a happier time than had her sister. She reached a level of acceptance, of contentment. Even though she could not do many things she had previously enjoyed, her life continued to have meaning.

Many, if not most, of those I talked with said that finding ways to adapt to change is necessary for aging well. But the strategies they employed varied from person to person.

Mary R, who is 80, tries to look squarely at what she is facing and make decisions based on that assessment:

> For instance, I know that I will never again put my feet in downhill skis, and I recently decided probably the same is true of cross-country skiing, because I just don't want to fall.
>
> My approach is if something becomes physically impossible or unachievable, I look for something else. You look around and see, "OK, is this something that's easy to replace in my life? Is it something I can happily do without? What do I need to do to find something that adequately replaces it?" For instance, I'm having a lot of trouble with my right shoulder, and swimming used to be a physical activity I really enjoyed. Right now, I just could not do that unless I could figure out a one-armed stroke, which I suppose I might be able to do. But what I know I will do next summer is get a membership at the municipal pool where they have a "lazy river," which gives you really good exercise walk-

ing against the current of the river. I suppose there are some things that happen that you cannot deal with in that way—at least, I suppose there are—but I haven't given those much thought, to be perfectly honest.

When I contacted Mary a year after this interview, she caught me up on what she had been doing: "I should report that last October I became bionic with a new right shoulder, so I'm back in the swimming business—among other things!"

She told me about another adaptation which had to do with changing circumstances other than physical infirmity. She and her husband had developed a family tradition of celebrating New Year's Eve—put the children to bed early, fix a really fancy dinner, dress up, and light candles.

As the children grew older, they wanted to be in on the celebration too, so then they would dress up as well. Mary and her husband fixed a fancy dinner for their children, serving them as if in a restaurant. Then she and her husband would clean up the kitchen before dressing up themselves—and then the children would serve them. It became a family tradition, observed even when their children were college students.

But then Mary's husband died, and their customary New Year's Eve practice no longer worked. So she decided to create a new tradition:

> What I did was invite people over. Some years it was for dinner; some years it was dessert. I would ask them to bring a favorite thing they liked to read and then they all took turns reading out loud. Some people brought things they had written; most people brought things they really just loved. It was a very fulfilling kind of evening and

totally different from what we had done before. It pre-
vented the nostalgia from becoming "Oh, woe is me."

Others reported a variety of adaptations they have made
when faced with loss or diminished capacities.

John G noted that when his back went out, he and his wife
learned to lean against each other for mutual support. "We
adapted," he said, "by becoming closer." They held each other up.

Bob H spoke of his wife who had an autoimmune disease
and required dialysis. They refused to let it curtail the activities
they wanted to pursue. When they decided to visit Yellowstone
National Park, they took the dialysis machine with them. They
flew to Rapid City, South Dakota, drove to Yellowstone, and
arranged to have the fluids she needed shipped to them at stops
along the way. "So, we did that," he said, "and it was fine."

A chaplain who serves residents in another retirement community remembers a conversation with a resident who said, "I
moved to Colorado because hiking and the mountains were so
important to me. In my first living will, I wrote that if I can't
hike and climb anymore, don't do life-extending things: just
keep me comfortable. But now I'm in my 70s; hiking is not so
damned important to me anymore!"

Another woman, also a mountain climber, said, "Finally,
it just dawned on me. I didn't leave anything up there in the
mountains that I have to go get. I have learned to look at them
and have appreciation for what they look like and know what
they're like up there, but I don't have to go there anymore."

Gail T used to own her own business. She had to give it up
but transferred what she liked about it into another realm. She
loves "designing systems," and she has found her church to be
a system in need of redesign.

She observed that in making adaptations, it is important to "keep your eye on the quality of your life. That's the goal. It isn't to get over whatever this infirmity is; it's to maintain quality of life for as long as you can." That's what the "equipment" of old age is for: canes, walkers, wheelchairs, scooters. They're about doing what we can to maintain quality of life, both physically and emotionally.

Susan H admitted that the extra effort required to make such accommodations can wear her down, and sometimes she feels defeated. She remembered her discouragement when she realized that she couldn't safely negotiate the stairs at a professional sports facility, which made it unwise for her to attend. "I'm disappointed," she said, "but so what? I'll go to the Kennedy Center and see a symphony. You have to find a Plan B."

Change is inherent to life. While just about everybody already knows that, coming to terms with the reality of these changes challenges—just about everybody. We hold on tightly to what is and are surprised when "what is" does not prove to be permanent.

We might try to identify an anchor, something that holds true—a belief, a hope, an ideal to strive for—even when everything around is in flux. That is one approach. Another is plain old denial. A man in his early 80s told me that sometimes he forgets how old he is, because "I don't feel any different." Then he goes out and does things he shouldn't—and pays for it later with a strained muscle, or he just gets exhausted. Others tell me how young they look, how surprised I would be to learn their real age. Well, maybe.

But in my everyday interactions with seniors who remain active participants in life, I find my truest guides are those who ride the changes lightly: accept them gracefully and make adaptations. They seek what is available and possible in the new reality they encounter each day of their lives.

I am reminded of how I learned to ride a roller coaster. My friend in the sixth grade, Jimmy, advised me to hold tight and scream. It didn't work. All that grasping and screaming made me even more tense. My muscles ached, and my throat hurt. A better strategy was to relax into it. Accept that I was being taken for a ride that I did not control. Bend and adapt.

1.
What changes have you experienced as you have aged?

2.
Do you generally welcome change? Resist change? Some combination of the two? Give an example of how you have responded to a change in your life.

3.
What adaptations to change have you observed in others? In yourself? Which have been successful? Which not?

4.
Looking ahead, how would you like to address the changes that you encounter? What do you want your attitude to be?

THREE

Identity

*All of a sudden, you find you're not
the center of attention anymore.*
—Dick B, age 85

"Who am I?"

Identity has to do with one's sense of self. It grounds us in the world. How do I view myself? How do others regard me? How can I be faithful to the person I am? How do I know when I veer from this path? What is distinctive about me?

The trouble is, identity changes, just like everything else. "Who I am" grows, evolves, diminishes, and deepens in waves throughout our lives. Once we think we've got ourselves figured out, conditions change, and we have to amend our sense of who we are—again. Sometimes, too, we are surprised by how we react to a situation and what it reveals about ourselves. "I didn't know I had that in me. I didn't realize that is part of who I am."

Perhaps my identity is grounded in how I look. That changes. Who am I when my hair turns gray or white and thins, when I develop wrinkles, when I don't stand as tall as I once did, when my body thickens? "I hate looking in the mirror," one woman said. "I don't see any of *me* there." Where is the "me" we are looking for in the mirror?

Perhaps my identity is tied up with what I can do. These might be strenuous pursuits: playing tennis, running a marathon, scaling a mountain, chopping wood, climbing a ladder to clean leaves from the gutters. Or more ordinary activities: walking, going up or down a flight of stairs, keeping pace with a companion, getting up from a chair, breathing easily. An 87-year-old woman reported, "Four or five years ago, I turned a corner into age. Before that, I was swimming every day. *Every day*. And I remember walking very, very, very rapidly and being proud of the comments people would make: 'Oh, look at you go. I wish *I* could.' I was showing off. Now I'm so ashamed." Who am I once I can't swim daily, walk rapidly, if I need a walker or a scooter to make my way through the world?

Perhaps my identity is derived from my role in the family. I'm the mom; I'm the dad. My family looks to me to keep their lives organized and running smoothly. They need me to provide income that supports the family, wisdom to offer direction, communication to keep us in relationship with each other, cooking to feed us, love to nourish our self-worth and sustain us through hard times. Others in my family look to me, depend upon me. But that too changes as our children become independent, acquire skills beyond what we possess, start their own families, make decisions, fashion their own lives.

Perhaps my identity depends on my place in the world. Once I was an important person. Others looked to me for advice and guidance. I possessed skills that others needed; I had access to information that others valued. I had power. People paid attention when I spoke and sought my favor. But now I feel invisible. People don't seek me out, don't listen to what I have to say. So now, without the power and position I once possessed, who am I?

Barbara L told me about taking her stepmother to dinner: "The waitress talked to me, but not to her—she was invisible. And my stepmother was looking at her with absolute daggers, like, wait a minute, I am here, talk to *me*." Who am I if others look past me, regard me as a lesser person, don't take my thoughts and feelings into account? Barbara L noted that she sees herself as a "pretty vibrant 75-year-old." Even so, she has noticed that younger people have started calling her "dear." "Please don't call me 'dear.' I have a *name*!"

A social worker told me about a couple in their late 80s in which the woman has always been in charge of the house and has always been the primary caregiver. She has prepared the meals, made the schedules for the family, kept things picked up and in order, and provided emotional support. That's been her identity for more than sixty years. Recently, her attention has been focused on her husband, who has needed more and more help. But now she too is becoming frail. It is difficult to do what she has always done, to be who she has always been. Maybe she cannot continue to be as involved in his care. Maybe she can no longer be responsible for everything she has done in the family.

But her identity is that she is the one who manages the details, and she is the caregiver. This is who she has always been. Furthermore, her children, who have always seen her in this role, have a difficult time letting it go. "You're Mom," they say. "It's your job to take care of Dad." Maybe they need to pay an aide to take on some of the everyday tasks. They have money, so that's not an issue. But here, the woman resists. "I can't imagine paying someone. That's *my* responsibility."

And so they take no action. This woman may die taking care of her husband, taking care of her family. She will cling to that identity even if it literally kills her. She can't imagine giving it up without surrendering her own sense of being. This particular woman is not the only person who faces this dilemma. I have observed both women and men who—consciously or unconsciously—make that decision. They cling to their identity even when it puts their own health at risk.

Susan H spoke of having to adjust her sense of who she was when she realized that her position in the family had changed:

> I guess the biggest surprise—it shouldn't have been a surprise but it's something I had a hard time getting my mind around—is that I was no longer the head of a family, that my son and daughter-in-law, and my daughter and son-in-law—those are *their* families, and each of them is the head of their own family. I'm not in charge, and I think it took a little adjustment for me to get to that. I thought, you know, I thought that I *should* be. Because I'd always been Mom, right? I thought Sunday dinners at my house would never end. Well, of course they did. As my children's kids get older, they want Sunday dinner at their house. That's perfectly all right.

It was not easy for her to relinquish what had been her role in the family. But as she opened herself to the reality of this change, she discovered unexpected benefits and gifts. She was surprised to learn that when she let go of her identity as head of the family, something else opened up, "in lovely ways." She remarked, "You let go of control and you gain such a warmth, and it's nice to be welcomed with open arms, not because they have to, not because you know everything or have all the money, but because they *like* you. It's my privilege and honor to be welcomed in."

Susan's initial surprise and, perhaps, some feelings of hurt came from her realization that her place in the family—her place in the world—had changed. It took some getting used to; she had to shift her identity to different foundations. But once she was able to accept the change, something new opened. She discovered that she is valued not just because of her role as Mom but because people in her family appreciate her as a person and like her for who she is.

Dick B, who spent his professional career in radio and television broadcasting, retired when he was 75. He was 85 when I interviewed him. He told me of the losses he and his wife had experienced. "We've lost a lot of friends. We've lost family members. Brothers and sisters, both of us, my wife and I. Physically, sure, I have aches and pains. It takes 'a groan and a half' to get out of a chair. . . . Work was a major, major part of my life, and going away from it was a loss." And now, when the family gets together, he finds that he's on the periphery of conversations. "They're not interested so much in what I think." That, he said, has been a surprise.

Who am I when my professional life ends? Who am I if my opinions are not sought, if I have a hard time entering the conversations occurring among those of younger generations? I may have spent my lifetime developing skills and relationships that have defined my place in the world. Who am I when those skills are no longer relevant, no longer wanted, and when the relationships fade?

Since retirement, Dick has found ways to "reinvent" himself and revise his sense of who he is. He began teaching English to immigrants, Hispanics especially. That provided opportunities to be involved with other people, to make contributions to their lives. Maybe he didn't have the power or the visibility he had enjoyed when in broadcasting, but he could still make a difference. "Boy, I loved it," he recalled of his teaching. "I'd never taught before, and it was great. It was very rewarding." Teaching helped him discover and develop a new role for himself. It brought him a new identity.

That also ended when driving at night became a problem, and Dick wasn't able to get to the location where the classes were held. So he found a center closer to home and took on yet another role. "What I do now is conduct what they call 'conversation club classes' at the local library. People come in, and we talk. We talk in English. They get to practice their English. We don't teach them language. If they make a bad mistake, I correct them, but it's not a teaching course. The idea is to speak in English and get some practice doing it."

Dick's identity was once grounded in his work as a broadcaster with a worldwide audience. But now it has shifted. Now his sense of who he is comes less from the recognition he enjoyed earlier, more from helping others one on one, enabling them to develop language skills so that they can establish their own place in the world. Who am I now? I am a person who makes a difference in other people's lives; I participate in the life of a community.

Barbara L spoke of how difficult it is to maintain a positive sense of self in our culture that focuses on younger people, while ignoring (or ridiculing) older people. "I look at television ads and they're geared mostly to that 18-to-49-year-old demographic. I hate it! It's really hard because I think, as much as I don't like it, when you get older, you are marginalized."

She told me about seeing an ad for a "real cute dress" on television that morning. "And I thought, 'God, that's the kind of dress I used to wear.' It made me sad. It was fleeting, but there was a moment when there was a little pang of, 'Oh my goodness, that's the kind of dress I used to look really cute in. Sure couldn't wear that now.'" But then, she said, her humor kicked in. She laughed and cited "the spandex rule"—"*Just because you can, doesn't mean you should.* So it's fleeting. 'That's such a cute dress, and I know I could still wear it, but I'd look like a complete idiot.' So it's hard to maintain a sense of self."

Barbara P's career as a software engineer and mathematician was a source of engagement, challenge, satisfaction, and identity. She entered the field at a time when there were few women in it. She remembers going to career counseling before entering college. "They told me I could do anything I wanted." But "they" also told her that 50 percent of women who became engineers didn't get married. And 50 percent of those who married didn't have children. "Terrible odds," she concluded.

Nevertheless, Barbara persisted, earned a degree, married, and—with the help of her husband—landed a job with the government. "I was typically the only woman in the branch," she said. "I was very lucky. I had a very wonderful career in determining gravity models and plate tectonics and tides." She rose to the level of manager and then became the branch head. Also, further defying the odds, she had children, staying at home with them for two and a half years. It wasn't easy to balance all that, but she had a supportive husband who realized

that Barbara needed to work—to have a career in a field that
she cared about—in order to live at peace with herself.

Then she began having problems hearing. "We were at
these big tables, and I couldn't hear what was going on. They
didn't accommodate me, and I had to force them to get me
an amplified telephone." Ultimately, she retired early because,
with her poor hearing, she couldn't perform at the level she
considered necessary to do her job.

This was difficult. "At one point, I was this big manager; I
had a hundred people who were dependent on me. And then,
all of a sudden, nobody cared about me anymore. And I didn't
have the respect I had in that position. Basically, I had to build
my own—what I considered to be respect."

In retirement, she has sought other ways to establish an
identity. She prepares taxes as a volunteer for those in need of
such assistance. As a software engineer and mathematician, she
finds offering that service a natural way to use her skills. "I'm
saving them a lot of money. I also help people who are learning
how to use computers. If somebody needs one-on-one, I'll do
that." She has become an advocate for those with hearing loss,
taking on some big targets. Netflix, for instance. She wasn't able
to read the captioning on Netflix movies because the lettering
was white and not visible when there was a light background.
Newer TVs offer options that address the problem, but these
options aren't available on older models. So she contacted Netflix and asked them to change the captions. "They refused to
do it," she reported. So then "I contacted the Department of
Justice, and very quickly thereafter, they got changed!"

Barbara has drawn upon her training and aptitude as a
mathematician and her knowledge of systems and how they
can be changed, as well as a new sensitivity for what it takes

for those with diminished capacities to negotiate everyday life. Because of the accommodations she has had to make for herself, she has an understanding of—and compassion for—not only those with hearing impairments, but those experiencing a reduction in powers and abilities they might have previously taken for granted. "Oh, and I also know that people don't know what it's about until they're going through it."

This has enabled her to craft an identity different from that of her earlier years but that draws upon knowledge gained throughout her life, which she applies to situations she now faces. To address the question "Who am I?" she has developed a self-image that is new but connected to her previous identity.

In reflecting upon the evolution of her sense of self, Barbara offers this advice to those who are looking ahead to their own aging: "Make sure you have other interests besides your job. Because you relate very heavily to that position; that's you, especially if you are successful at the job. You suddenly cut that off, and you have a real disconnect. You have to find some other way to get your self-image."

In modern Western society, identity derives primarily from one's sense of self as an individual: what I look like, what I can do, the accomplishments I can claim, the roles I play in everyday life, the resources I control, the power I can exert. We may also derive a sense of self from the communities in which we participate, but such collective identity is usually secondary. So while my identity is influenced by my family, the town in which I live, my faith community, my ethnic heritage, and my football team, personal identity tends to weigh more heavily than any of these.

But as we age, personal identity may diminish in importance, and we identify more strongly with our communities of heritage and/or communities of choice. Marguerite R reported her growing appreciation of the legacy she receives as a person of Greek ancestry. Her own identity is enriched through participating in the flow of Greek culture and history; it's an important part of who she is. So the foundations of our identity may shift from the personal to the collective, which, in turn, helps forge a deeper sense of who we may be.

Kate L remembered that as a young person, she broke from her community of heritage as a Jew, and she claimed the right to establish her own place in the world. "I was 14. I had too much Manischewitz wine at a Seder. I looked around and thought, 'Who *are* these people?'" As a young person, she sought to unburden herself of what she considered the limitations her Jewish heritage imposed upon her. At that stage of her life, Jewishness seemed less a resource and more an impediment to making a life on her own terms. "I rebelled," she said. "Oh, I rebelled. When I was 17, on Yom Kippur, I had a ham and cheese sandwich. How's *that* for rebellion?"

And for much of her life, she had little connection with a Jewish faith community. But now, she returns. Those she dismissed at the Seder when she was 14—"these people"—now give foundation to her sense of a place in the world, and she reports her "tremendous feeling about being Jewish":

> I go to Sabbath services in the morning because I can't go at night. I'm too tired, so I go to the morning thing. And a big reason for going is, oh man, how sweet it is to remember how to read Hebrew and sing the songs nice and loud, and I do. I do! And that's satisfying. That's gratifying.

It's not so much faith as it is people-hood and nationhood. I'm so proud to be a Jew. I so love being Jewish. I love the music. I love the history. I love the language. I'm writing poetry in Yiddish now. It's my first language.

Family can also be a source of collective identity. One woman spoke with joy about a practice her family has developed —a dinner together each Sunday evening from 5:00 until 7:00 p.m. The generations gather in one home or another for that two-hour period. They share a meal, they talk about what's going on in their lives, they stay in contact. So the family history and the family values remain alive and vital. As we grow older, that becomes more important: Who am I? I am part of a particular family that extends through the generations. As I near the end of my life, my sense of who I am shifts to a larger context: not just me, but the ongoing story of my family and its involvement in the world. This woman said with satisfaction that the values she and her husband have sought to live by now are being expressed in new ways by the younger generations in their family.

Another source of collective identity can be found in those who stay abreast of their field of expertise, even as they, themselves, are no longer actively involved. I became acquainted with a man who had devoted his life to working for union organizations, at both the local and national levels. When I met him, he was in his 80s and had been retired for many years, but he kept current on the issues he had always followed. I found him a valuable source of information, insight, and perspective in his field of expertise. Especially perspective. He was able to place current events in the context of what had come before.

He could point out dangers and possibilities; he identified the meanings of what was happening now in a way that those with a shorter frame of reference could not. Now his identity was rooted less in his own role in creating and implementing policy and more in offering a long-term view of the development of unionization: its challenges, its possibilities.

Several people spoke to me about their involvement in civil rights work over the years. There have been setbacks, certainly, but also progress. Those who lived in Washington, D.C., spoke of the severe segregation in that city during their lifetime and how they took part in efforts to dismantle the structures that supported racism and helped build a society that would support equal rights and equal access. They participated in boycotts of segregated restaurants, outreach to bring together communities of shared values, efforts to understand the life experiences of those who appeared to be quite different, and demonstrations aimed at bringing injustices to the attention of a wider public. A woman spoke of taking an overnight train to the 1963 March on Washington for Jobs and Freedom. She had spent the night singing "freedom songs" with others bound for the demonstration. On the next day, when the pinnacle moment of the demonstration came—Martin Luther King Jr.'s "I Have a Dream" speech—she was so exhausted that she had fallen fast asleep under a tree. Nevertheless, she forged her identity through a lifetime of commitment to the ideals of a just and open society.

Joyce T told of a trip she took with her family when she was a child: African Americans from the North, entering the South. The family car broke down soon after they had crossed the Mason-Dixon line, and they took it to the Buick dealership for repairs. The service department put them at the end of the priority line with the implicit message, "We'll get to it . . . after we fix the white people's cars." This was not likely to happen until the next day, so her family of five faced an overnight in this community where they didn't know anyone and where the hotels did not admit "colored" people.

Joyce remembers her aunt saying, "Stay here. I'm going for a walk." She was gone for a less than an hour. Upon returning, she carried a house key. She had found an African-American woman who invited them to stay in her home for the night. This woman had to work, so she gave Joyce's aunt the key to her home and invited them to let themselves in. The next morning, the woman made breakfast for the five travelers and refused to take any money until Joyce's family insisted that their gift would be a contribution to her church.

This was a story of survival, how people who have been systematically denied the basic services of society found a way to support each other. But it was also a story of identity: how being part of a community—a people—can be just as important to one's identity as who one is as an individual. Many years later, when, presumably, such blatant discrimination would no longer occur, that early experience remains with Joyce, reminding her of her identity as a member of a people whose history and culture have sustained them for generations.

As we age, personal identity may diminish in importance. What can replace it is a sense of participating in something larger than ourselves and a longer frame of reference than our own lifetime. We can step back from everyday involvement and see our role as part of an ongoing story of our people, our family, our realm of expertise.

Dementia presents a particular challenge in retaining a sense of identity. We may lose our ability to think clearly and express ourselves. Short term memory may become less reliable: what I did yesterday, who visited me this morning, what I ate for lunch or whether I had lunch. For some people, long term memory is also affected, and we lose track of events which have occurred throughout our lives. We don't remember our work or the causes we devoted ourselves to. We might not recognize friends or even family members. As a result, people with dementia sometimes fill in the blanks of their memories with imagined experiences. A woman who had a long and productive career as a teacher and had raised six children told me that she had never married, had no children, never held a job. At other times, though, she did remember aspects of her history, who she had been and, from that, who she was.

In my experience, most people with dementia retain a sense of who they are even as both short-term and long-term memories fade. They are still very much the same person, with the same personality and the same outlook on life, even when the specifics of their own history become less available to them. A person with a sunny outlook on life retains that orientation even as it becomes harder to think and remember. Or a person who has always had an interest in technology retains his enthusiasm at encountering what is to his memory a new gadget, even though he might have seen and used it many times before. But this is not always the case. Sometimes there are severe personality changes.

A woman spoke of her father, who had been superintendent of schools in their community. He was deeply involved in local politics and civic redevelopment projects and concluded his career as dean of students at a small college. Her father was a person of stature in the community. But when he developed Alzheimer's disease, he became delusional and then extremely angry.

His wife transferred him to a nursing home because she could no longer care for him herself. At first, he did well in the new setting and told visitors of imagined adventures. "In his view," his daughter said, "an airplane landed each morning that would take him and other residents on an excursion. He had the responsibility of getting his roommates up and dressed so they could come along. Then the plane took them all over the world, landing back at their facility—in time for dinner. (His daughter speculated that the proximity to an airport and the sound of airplanes taking off and landing may have brought him to create this story and his role in it.)

But as the disease progressed, this man became angry and fought with the aides when they tried to help him. He interpreted every touch as an assault; he would fight them, hit them. He lost track of the person he had been.

As some people age, they lose access to their memories, their capacity to interact with others diminishes, and their personality may change. They may lose the ability to use reason in solving everyday problems that would have been quite simple for them before they became afflicted with dementia. This does not happen to everyone. Everyone does lose some mental capacity in aging: remembering names, thinking of the word you want to say, forming memories of recent experiences. But not everyone is subject to dementia.

The challenge for the family who loves someone who is severely affected, and for the caregivers who seek to be of service: How do we effectively care for this person and how do we communicate the love that we feel? How can we make a difference at this stage of life? How can we help?

1.

How has your identity—your sense of who you are—changed as you have grown older?

2.

How do you think other people's views of you may have changed?

3.

In addition to your personal identity, do you have a sense of participating in a larger community: an ethnic heritage, a people, those working for a cause, a professional field, an extended family? How do these affect your sense of who you are?

4.

Have you ever held on too long to a part of your identity? Have you ever surrendered it too quickly?

FOUR

Help

*I've said things to you today that
I haven't discussed with anybody else.*
—Joyce T, age 95

Those preparing for the ministry are required to take a course in chaplaincy, during which they work in a hospital or other health care setting and interact with patients. This is almost always a defining experience in the life of a seminary student. One moves from the theoretical to the actual, confronting the essential question of how one human being can make a difference to others, particularly those who face challenges to their health and may be suffering. Each student in that first experience of chaplaincy must consider, "How can I help?"

My own chaplaincy training took place in a hospital for the incurably ill in Massachusetts. Residents of this institution experienced a variety of conditions, all of which were considered to be incurable. But "incurable" is not the same as "termi-

nal." Many of them would live for years with the condition that
brought them to be hospitalized. Some of them, with proper
support, would have been able to live in a non-institutional
setting. The real common denominator among the residents of
this institution was that they had no place else to go.

In this setting, what could I do that would matter? I
couldn't cure these people. I couldn't materially improve their
lives. I had my own doubts about salvation, however it might
be defined, so I couldn't offer that as an escape. It wasn't clear to
me what I might have to give as I talked with people, making
my way from bed to bed.

The chaplaincy program in which I participated featured
regular meetings in a small group with others enrolled in the
course. This gave us opportunities to reflect on our experiences, raise questions, express doubts. At one such meeting,
I described a conversation I'd had the day before with a man
in his early 90s of French Canadian descent. He had suffered
a series of small strokes, whose primary effect was that he
sometimes spoke French without realizing it wasn't English.
Otherwise, he seemed to be a reasonably active and healthy
old man. On some days, he seemed to enjoy opportunities
to converse, often returning to a favorite topic: "the Blond
Bomber." The way he laughed after pulling out that name
suggested an old girlfriend or a long-ago encounter, though
he wouldn't go into details.

His demeanor was quite different, though, on this particular day when I stopped by to talk. He was feeling low.
He knew he was not getting out of this hospital. He had no
place to go; he had no people to go to. He was feeling his age,
wondering what was ahead for him. He sounded discouraged;
he looked sad.

As I reported back to my small group of fellow students, I didn't know what to say. I didn't think I had anything to offer. I had no idea how I could help.

"Okay," my supervisor said. "Let's role-play."

"Oh, God," I thought. "I hate to role-play." I suspected that my supervisor didn't know what to do either, but in his bag of tricks he could always pull out the "let's role-play" option.

So my supervisor became the man I had spoken with the previous day, while I played myself.

"How are you today?" I said. "Oh, not so good," replied my supervisor, and he proceeded to recite the worries I had reported from my account of the real conversation.

Again, I did not know what to say. I didn't have solutions; there was nothing I could do to change the conditions of his life. So I concentrated on being there with him as he proceeded along his lonely journey. I just wanted him to know that he wasn't alone.

At the end of our role-playing, the supervisor reached over, touched me on the shoulder, and said, "Good, Bruce. I felt ministered to."

Oh.

Maybe offering help is simpler—and more difficult— than I had thought. Maybe it doesn't have to involve solving problems for people or answering all their questions. Maybe it doesn't require fixing anything in their lives or cheering them up or trying to convince them that everything's going to be fine. Maybe what helps is more a matter of forming a connection with another person. Maybe it's being present, listening, valuing that individual. Maybe that is how we help.

As a chaplain in a senior residence community, I see many well-intentioned efforts at helping that come up short or fail outright. Just about all of these can be attributed to the same cause: failing to take into account the person we are trying to help. We let our own needs and desires drive us rather than pay attention to the other.

Roger M, a retired attorney in his early 90s, told a story that had a group of his contemporaries convulsed in the kind of laughter that comes from recognizing a situation as both ridiculous and true. Many of them, it seems, had similar experiences. This man's story concerned a chair. He had an easy chair where he sat to watch television, read, work on a crossword puzzle, or sometimes just be. He and his chair had been companions for a long time, and over the years it had adjusted to his body. So the two of them—man and chair—fit amicably together. Admittedly, the chair was showing its years, looking shabby, and it wasn't all that clean anymore. Nevertheless, Roger loved his chair.

Then one day, he arrived home and—the chair was gone! Replaced by a brand new easy chair: beautiful and shiny and equipped with premium features like motorized leg rests and a headrest that tilts into any conceivable position. When you want to sit, you press a button, and the chair rises to meet you. When you want to get up, it lifts and gently sends you on your way.

This man's children had decided that the old chair had to go and so they replaced it, as a surprise. Well. Roger agreed that the new chair was a lot more attractive and had more features than his old chair could have ever imagined. Except . . . it wasn't comfortable. It hadn't put in the years necessary to become truly acquainted with its owner. This chair wasn't *his* chair.

But it didn't feel right to complain. His children had delivered the new chair with good intentions. They had wanted to do something nice for their father, and they were actually quite pleased with themselves. In their view, they had rid their father's apartment of an eyesore and possible health hazard (hard to know what was living in the crevices of that old chair!), and they had transported Roger into the modern age of cutting-edge easy-chair technology. Each time one of them visited, they could view this exhibit of how much they loved him.

Roger concluded that it would be too grumpy for him to express reservations about this gift, so he smiled and thanked his children. Besides, his beloved old chair was probably residing in a dump somewhere. It wasn't coming back.

And yet, he confided to this group of seniors who nodded in appreciation of his dilemma, "I *hate* that new chair!"

In seeking to help another—loved one, friend, or stranger—our actions are guided by our own perceptions of another's situation in life and what, from our perspective, we think this other person may want and need. Or *should* want and need. The result might be a new chair—because *I* certainly wouldn't want to sit on that old thing. Or pressure to take a pottery class—I would love to learn how to throw a pot, and you should too. Or a surprise party for your next birthday— you're 90, so celebrate! *I'll* want to celebrate if *I* make it to 90. Or a covert housecleaning—because *I* certainly wouldn't want to live that way. We make assumptions about what someone should want and need, and we act on that basis.

This evades the hard work of relationship: taking time to be present to another, listening, sharing one's own thoughts and feelings in response, asking questions, paying attention to what is said and accepting it, honoring it. In long-term relationships—like that of parent and child—we slip into habits of communication that may rarely stray from familiar patterns that have developed over years and decades. We may have been interacting with each other for forty, fifty, sixty years. It becomes hard to hear anything that doesn't fit with what has come before.

Instead of building an actual relationship, we insert what we *think* this person may want and need or what *we* want and need. For example, we may confront the elderly with an excess of cheerfulness. When you listen to visitors and staff talk to the residents of a retirement community, you could be forgiven for thinking that you're overhearing a kindergarten class—or a preschool. We speak in unnaturally lively tones, drawing on a vocabulary suitable for the very young. Or we encourage "activity." Be active! Join clubs! Start a new hobby! Take a course!

And then there are the publications aimed at seniors that are so resolutely chipper that I can barely read them. They appear to be written by young people who assume that relationships with the elderly should be about perkiness. "Hoof it for health!" shouts one article, on the protection against breast cancer afforded by brisk walking. "Protect your peepers!" proclaims another, on the advisability of taking care of our eyes. Couldn't we just say, "Take a walk?" and "Wear sunglasses?" Do we really have to get cutesy in order to attract the wandering attention of seniors?

The message that comes through these efforts is our own discomfort with aging. Jeff Watson, the director of operations at Erickson Living observed, "If we as younger people try to make our seniors look happy, talk happy—it's usually less for them and more for us. We like it better when they're happy. We think we're doing a good job when they are happy. We think it's our job to make them happy. And actually, if they don't make *us* happy by acting happy, we're unhappy with *them*."

Many seniors I interviewed admitted that they don't talk with their children about their deepest concerns because they fear that honesty might upset them. As one woman put it, "Our children don't want to hear us. It hurts them too much." And so they protect their children even as their children protect them. The generations don't connect. We pretend cheerfulness, offer distractions, assure each other that everything is "fine," because it's easier and less threatening than actually paying attention to each other.

The essential principle of what does help is simple: be present to other people as they are, not as you want them to be. This means putting aside your own needs and expectations so that you can pay attention to this actual human being who is right here, right now, in front of you. It means giving up on the project of "fixing" people or jollying them up and, instead, accepting them. It means regarding the elderly as human beings. Just that. Treating seniors as you want to be treated yourself: with respect and kindness.

While this is a simple formula, the actual practice can involve considerable trial and error. We will make mistakes, misread situations. We will frequently feel uncertain. This is not a bad thing. The tradition of contemplative spirituality urges us to enter new situations with openness, casting aside preconceptions, becoming "empty" so that we can be present to what is actually before us. Rather than entering with the assumption that we know what is good for the person we seek to serve, we assume an outlook of "not-knowing." And rather than approaching an encounter with the confidence that we know what we're doing, we empty ourselves. We become present.

For guidance on what someone can do to help another, I look to seniors themselves to point the way.

Bonnie K is 71. She speaks of visiting people who are more than twenty years older than she is. In these visits, she hopes to make connections with other people as she herself ages and encounters the inevitable losses. At this stage of life, she acknowledges, "It's hard to get to know people. It's hard to find people that you have things in common with." The new relationships she creates through her visits feed her need for human contact and for community.

She also cites a sense of mission to reach out to those who may be isolated, who cannot get out themselves. So she goes to them. "I see people in assisted living who are really pretty lonely."

But she wonders about what she can do. "I'm struggling with the issue of how I can help," she says. "I don't really have a sense about what I'm doing." She listens to the people she visits, lets them take the conversations where they want them to go, tries to respond to the conditions of each person's life. "One of the women is a newly widowed 94-year-old. Her husband died a couple months ago, and she's making the transition from independent to assisted living. She's confused and struggling right now. I help by getting her to meals. I end up talking to her about what's going on and who has visited her and what she needs to do that day. Another woman, who is also 94, is much more alert. She'll talk about her history, so I know a lot about her family, her career, her life in Europe, her nuclear family." Two different 94-year-old women, two different sets of needs, two different ways to help. For the first, she offers assistance with the basics of getting to a meal and helping her keep track of everyday occurrences. For the second, Bonnie makes herself available for conversation as this woman reflects upon the events of her life and weaves them together into stories.

Bonnie is surprised that she has formed close friendships with women whose husbands are very ill or have recently died. She is married, has not experienced that loss herself, but finds that those who have faced the illness and death of a spouse become more open to relationship. She speaks of a close friendship that developed with a woman she met when her husband was ill. For six months, Bonnie provided respite care so that this woman could take breaks and do errands that took her away from him. Another woman's husband died about a month ago, and the friendship between Bonnie and her has deepened since then. "There is something that bonds me with these women, because I've been through something with them when they've been through a really difficult time."

For Bonnie, a key has been living in the present. She developed this perspective when her own husband was going through cancer treatment. She said, "I learned how to live in the present through cancer. That's a cancer gift, and it was a total surprise. You cannot plan when somebody has cancer. You just have to go with the flow. I would never have expected I would be able to do that." Bonnie reported another surprise from the period her husband was in treatment: "We ended up laughing a lot!" This may be because laughter expresses defiance of the afflictions that keep us bound to our own concerns, tethering us to the ground. Laughter offers release, is an expression of freedom.

Yet caring for her husband during his cancer also exposed one of her own needs: "People would say to me all the time, 'How's Marty? How's Marty?' Nobody asked me how *I* was."

Rita D, who is 88, spoke of how she helps a neighbor in her retirement community who is experiencing mild dementia.

Rita looks out for her, helps her keep track of everyday activities, is available in case of emergency. "I have a neighbor down the hall who moved in at the same time I did and she now, well, she has had some senior senility and it's gotten worse, and I am concerned about her. I'll call her in the morning to make sure she remembers to meet me at a certain time and where we're going. She resents any help, but she needs it. Even eating with her, she has the shakes and so she can't really eat her soup. I ask them to bring it in a cup rather than a bowl because she never thinks to ask. You know, little things like that." She also has telephone numbers for the woman's children so they can be informed of anything that raises concerns.

Rita admits that helping this neighbor can be exasperating, particularly because she is very independent and resists help. She said,

> She had a heart attack, walked around for a week, her arm was sore. I asked, "Is it getting better?" "No." "Have you gone to the doctor?" "Well, it's fine." So finally, after a week, I called the daughter and told her. They came over, took her to the doctor, and she'd had a heart attack. She has a pacemaker now, but she's in denial about what she can and cannot do. I try to be a caregiver just to that extent. I mean, I'm not with her every day. We don't eat together every day, but she knows I'm here and if she has a question she calls me. People here know about her. And when you talk to her, you realize it. She's not quite all there. It could happen to me. It could happen to anybody, so I try to be tolerant.

How can we help? In this case, Rita is present for her friend. She is aware of the challenges facing this woman. She does small things that make this woman's life a little easier— calling to remind her about planned activities, making sure she has a cup for her soup, offering friendship even when "she's not quite all there." Those small actions are significant for this woman at this stage in her life.

I asked another woman, Ellen C, how family and friends might be able to help her and her husband at this stage in their lives. "Well," she said, "you can just come. Come and visit and make us a part of your lives. Tell us your problems. Listen to our stories. Tell us your life and listen to ours." Her husband is beginning to experience dementia and spends a lot of time putting together jigsaw puzzles, which he enjoys. "If anyone would come and work on the jigsaw puzzle with him, he would love it. They come and admire, but they don't participate."

It can be a challenge as we grow older to find activities that we can participate in. When we find something, it's helpful to share it. So come to visit, work on the jigsaw puzzle, show an interest in that person's world. Ellen spoke of a relative and her husband, who stop by to visit and play canasta, a card game, with them. It's appreciated. The two couples spend time together; they don't have to make conversation the whole time. It's a simple, easy activity. It keeps them in touch.

JoWynn J told me about her practice of visiting people in the assisted living section of her retirement community. She does this for her own benefit—to stay involved with people at a meaningful level. And she knows it helps those she visits, because they tell her so. "Even the ones who are in mild dementia thank me profusely, and they tell me how much they appreciate me coming every week. That's very good for me. I feel rewarded."

The people she visits mostly want to talk. "And I'm a good listener. I'm good at drawing people out. They talk about their lives, but they also talk about current events. They talk about events here in this community. They talk about their families."

JoWynn visits the same people every week so that they can build a relationship. "They get to know about me and my family, and I get to know about them. Right now, I'm visiting ten people: five on Tuesdays and five on Thursdays. It's good for me. It certainly is."

She told me about noticing that a former teaching colleague was in the assisted living section where she visits. "I had not been in touch with him since 1979, but I decided to see him; I just went to visit Stan." When she arrived, she found him nonresponsive. "They had him up in a wheelchair and dressed, but he had to be fed, and he was pretty much nonverbal. But his aide told me that he responded to music."

Many years before, Stan had introduced JoWynn to Verdi's *Requiem*. "So I took my boom box and a CD of the Verdi *Requiem* to play for him. And, Bruce, the tears started running down his cheeks. I was crying too. From then on I went every week, took a CD player and played different music for him. I played all kinds of music, different every week. I just sat with him in his room while we listened to the music."

Engaging in a conversation about aging can be intimidating. With our society's focus on the young, an underlying message comes through that it is not acceptable to get old, not even normal. Certainly nothing to talk about in polite company. We spend much of our lives trying not to age, denying that we are aging, devising strategies to stave it off. So when the time comes to consider the implications of getting older—for ourselves and for those around us—it can be difficult to break the habit of avoidance that has built up over a lifetime.

In my experience, many seniors want the opportunity to talk about their own aging: concerns, fears, plans that need to be made. But too often, attempts to start such a conversation are interrupted and diverted by another person's discomfort with the topic.

"I'm getting old," a person will venture. "My time is limited." "You're not getting old!" comes the reply. "I can barely keep up with you."

Or, "This is the last car I'll own. I'm not going to be here forever." The reply: "Nonsense! You'll outlive us all!"

Or, "I just realized I'm the same age as my father was when he died, older than my grandfather by twelve years." The reply: "But your health is so much better! And people live longer today—70 is the new 60!"

Each of these examples represents a missed opportunity. An elderly person is opening the door just a crack to address their own mortality. The responses, though, make it clear that the person being addressed is not comfortable talking about it. Rather than simply being present and listening, that person offers a forced optimism that diverts the exchange away from what the elderly person wants to talk about and into less threatening territory.

Seniors I have talked with also reported conversations shut down by a lack of sensitivity to what they might need. A woman told her friend about a death in the family that had hit her hard. The friend replied, in an offhanded manner, "Yeah, that's tough," which this woman experienced as a "brush-off," an unwillingness to acknowledge what she was experiencing. Another friend's first words upon seeing her during this time were "You look like hell!" Which, she admitted, was probably accurate but was not what she was looking for. "Others," she remembered, "were more in touch with their own emotions. They empathized, 'That's got to be really hard. This has got to be a hard one for you.'" When they spoke, she was able to relax and let herself be comforted.

When my wife was in treatment for breast cancer, I was terrified. I tried talking about what I was going through and caught a glimpse, I think, of what older seniors must experience on a regular basis. When I told a ministerial colleague I had known for decades about my wife's breast cancer, he responded, "My sister-in-law just died of that." Not quite what I was needing at the moment. Others just seemed very uncomfortable when I tried to talk about how my wife's illness was affecting me, and I quickly got the message that I was violating some unwritten rule governing appropriate conversation. I became very careful about who I shared information and feelings with. This, in turn, intensified my isolation during that very scary time.

Other people were helpful to me, and I learned from them about how I might respond in similar circumstances. The president of the congregation I then served reacted immediately when I told her about my wife's diagnosis. Her face expressed the shock and the horror I was feeling, and she said, "Oh! I am so sorry!" That and a hug. It was what I needed. Similarly, residents of the retirement community where I also served responded with concern—and not a lot of words. I didn't need much in the way of words. The care and concern are what mattered and what I remember now, seven years later.

I also remember that people in that retirement community told me about health conditions they faced that I had not known about previously. Several women talked with me about their own breast cancers, which I had not known about. And the man with whom I clashed in my initial interview for the chaplaincy position told me about a condition he lived with that was gradually sapping his strength and energy and that would likely lead to his own death. What mattered in these conversations were less the specifics of what others had faced than a sense that we were relating on a different level—a deeper level—than we had previously. That depth of connection was helpful and healing to me in the circumstances I then faced.

Mary R identified empathy as a quality that helps in facing the challenges of age:

> It's just like when you have anything that happens that makes you more empathetic with other people. That has happened with the aging process also. Once I got a small third-degree burn from boiling water, and just that experience and how it had to be dealt with med-ically and what it felt like made me more empathetic. You don't really understand unless you've experienced it yourself. And I think the same thing is true as you become less able to do things and you think, oh yeah, I remember this person I was helping, and I didn't really have the full effect of what this meant or how this felt. And now I do. You're always learning.

Joyce N observed, "You probably need one or two people who really care about you. And often it's not a blood relative. It's so important to have a few confidants who are really, really there for you." Joyce, who is 76, remembered an occasion when she received a call from someone in a support group they had both been in. This woman called: there had been an accident in which her 3-year-old had been injured. So Joyce went to the hospital where the woman was with her daughter and brought a teddy bear. "The mother was just so happy to see me! We chatted a bit. And I expressed my concern—what else can I do? And as I drove home that day I said, 'I do have strength. I do have energy. I just need to know where I can use it.'"

How can we help? Empathy. Patience. Presence. Being there. Listening. I asked Mildred R, who visits people in assisted living, about what helps when she visits. She said, "Smiling. Eye contact. A touch, not always but sometimes, when there's something particular going on; taking their hand and paying attention. Simple things. If they want to get a drink of water, I get it for them."

In talking with each other about aging, it helps to start simply. Begin difficult conversations with talk about easier things. It can be about what we've done today, yesterday, this week. It can be about the weather. We can have a conversation about a television show, a sports event—how your team is doing, the plants this person is caring for, pictures on the wall, photos framed on a bookshelf, a pet that wanders through the room. Consciously or not, we are always gauging how deep a conversation can go with each person: Can I trust you to talk about something that might be sensitive?

And then, if the atmosphere is right and if the person wants to explore a sensitive topic, you might sense an opening. A hint. People will often tell us what they need. Not directly, perhaps, but they will tell us what's on their mind, what they would like to talk about. "People need patience," Barbara L said of those who want to help. "P-A-T-I-E-N-C-E. They need to know how to say the right thing."

"Patience," Gail T said, echoing Barbara. "Be aware that when conversing with older people, you must be patient and wait for an answer to your question. Because the processing in the brain is slow—it doesn't mean they have dementia." We just slow down when we age.

Patience is also needed in listening for something that sounds heartfelt, that indicates a concern or a worry, that seems to come from a deeper place than everyday talk. And then the discipline to hold back whatever denials or reassurances pop into your mind. Indicate your willingness to be with a person who is struggling with the questions of the human condition that reside at the center of human existence: What does it mean for me to be old? What has been my place in the ongoing story that is human life? What might lie ahead?

But what about those we don't seem to be able to help? Then, perhaps, bearing witness is all we can do. JoWynn J told of one such experience among those she visited:

> I have told you about people who are very content in their old age. But I also befriended a woman who lived in my building, just downstairs from me. She was negative about everything. It was so hard for me to be with her, but I knew how unhappy she was and how desperate for company. So I would invite her up to my apartment about once a week, just to visit. And when she was hospitalized and had surgery, I went to the hospital every day. She died as a result of the surgery, but for ten days, I was there with her.

JoWynn told of trying to ease this woman's unhappiness, such as by urging her to try medication to address her depression. But she was not willing. Ultimately, JoWynn concluded, "She didn't become any happier because I was visiting with her every week." And yet, presence has value. Witness has value. When you stand with another person even during hard times, you affirm that person's worth. Your being there might not change that person's life, but it matters. It is enough.

While doing research for this book, I was surprised at how easy it was to find people willing to be interviewed about their own aging. At the beginning, I put out a few notices, but after that, people volunteered. About a quarter of the interviews were with residents of the retirement community where I work. Others came from a wide area—many from metropolitan Washington, D.C., but others from farther afield: Colorado, Michigan, Iowa, Minnesota. Since most of my interviews were conducted by phone, it didn't matter where they were. About half of those I interviewed were associated with a Unitarian Universalist congregation; the other half represented other faith communities.

After the interviews—which lasted from half an hour to an hour or more—the interviewees often thanked me for talking with them. As one woman put it, "This conversation has been so nice. We don't offer each other the opportunity for these kinds of conversations." Another reported that thinking about the interview made her focus on "how grateful I am for the life I have." Elaine S observed, simply, "We don't talk about aging, ever." And after an interview that went for more than ninety minutes, a woman apologized for how talkative she had been: "I'm afraid I probably burned your ears off! It was really very nice of you, because unless I talk to myself, I don't really have anybody to think about those things with anymore."

The way people have responded to my just offering them the opportunity to talk tells us something about what can help. It also reveals a lack in many people's lives as they grow older—someone who is available for conversations about things that matter to us, someone to be present, listen, share experiences. Someone who will accompany us on our journey, hear our stories, let us wonder out loud about this life in which we find ourselves. A companion along the way.

When I was a child, I spent summer evenings riding my bicycle up and down the sidewalks of my neighborhood. Mr. Cherry and his two sisters—all three elderly—lived together a few houses away from us. On warm nights, they sat outside on well-worn chairs on their front porch, seeking relief from the heat of the day that had built up inside. When I spotted them, I would direct my bike up their walk, pay them a visit. I don't remember what we talked about. I do remember that they were interested in me. They had time to pay attention to what I said; they weren't busy, heading off to something else. I remember that they smiled, and they laughed with me at things I told them. I felt valued.

The last time I saw Mr. Cherry was several years after my days of bike riding on neighborhood sidewalks. He was walking in the alley that connected several homes, including his and ours. I greeted him, and he smiled as he always did when he saw me—but also seemed troubled. He tried to ask me something, but I didn't understand. So I walked with him, and then realized that he was asking for help in finding his way home. He was lost just a few steps from the house in which he had lived for decades. At about the time this dawned on me, he saw something familiar that reoriented him. He laughed a little at his confusion and then continued on his way. I noticed that he walked differently than I remembered before: hunched over, slower, walking unevenly and carefully, rather than with the smoother gait of young people.

Later I learned that he had been institutionalized in a mental hospital and died soon thereafter.

I was slow to recognize what I saw when I encountered Mr. Cherry that day in the alley. I didn't know it was possible for a person to get lost in his own neighborhood, and it was disconcerting to see the changes coming over my old friend. Still more unsettling were comments I overheard from others in the neighborhood. That as his mental condition deteriorated, he had mistreated his sisters, which was why he had been committed to the mental institution. It was hard for me to accept that this gentle old man who had talked and laughed with me could mistreat anyone.

I remember his smile of recognition the last day I saw him, his asking for my help, even though I was clumsy in responding. And our walking together—not long, just enough for him to remember where he was, to find his way. I like to think that on that day, by walking with him, I was able to help.

1.

Identify an occasion when someone has helped you through a difficult time. What was it that helped?

2.

Can you name a time when you have been able to help someone else? What have you learned from that experience? What did you do that might help others as well?

3.

Can you think of occasions when you have tried to help another person, and it didn't work? Is there anything you might have done that would have been more effective?

4.

If someone were to ask you today, "How can I help?" what would you say? Would you like the opportunity to talk further about your own aging?

Meaning

I was probably feeling like I needed to prove
that my life had meant something.
—Mildred R, age 88

The fundamental human characteristic, according to Viktor Frankl, is our possession of a "will to meaning." This will to meaning, he said, provides us with our primary motivation for living. Without a sense that our life matters, we struggle. But if we do believe that our life makes a difference, we can survive hard times and extreme circumstances. Jeff Watson of Erickson Living expressed it this way: "Suffering all by itself may not destroy you, but suffering without meaning will."

Perhaps your life matters because you have made contributions to the lives of others—family, friends, or strangers. Perhaps you have devoted your life to becoming competent in your area of specialty, to learning in your field. Or perhaps a sense of mission has given meaning to your life; you seek to make a difference while guided by, living by, a set of values. Even if your mission has not been realized to the degree you had hoped, it still brings form and direction to your life. That is, it has given you meaning.

Frankl observed that meaning is essential no matter how our lives are proceeding—in good times and bad. Prosperity and accomplishment, in themselves, turn out to be empty goals without an underlying sense of purpose. But we especially need the conviction that our lives matter when we are under duress.

In *Man's Search for Meaning*, Frankl described an occasion during his imprisonment in a Nazi concentration camp that was particularly harrowing. And yet, despite the misery to which he was subject, it prompted a realization. Frankl was on a forced march with other inmates in the dark and cold, brutally prodded along by guards who did not hesitate to beat those who did not march smartly enough. "We stumbled on in the darkness, over big stones and through large puddles, along the one road leading from the camp. The accompanying guards kept shouting at us and driving us with the butts of their rifles."

A companion commented that he was glad their wives could not see them in this condition. Frankl writes,

> That brought thoughts of my own wife to mind. And as we stumbled on for miles, slipping on icy spots, supporting each other time and again, dragging one another up and onward, nothing was said, but we both knew: each was thinking of his wife.
>
> Occasionally I looked at the sky, where the stars were beginning to spread behind a dark bank of clouds. But my mind clung to my wife's image, imagining it with an uncanny acuteness. I heard her answering me, saw her smile, her frank and encouraging look. Real

or not, her look was then more luminous than the sun which was beginning to rise.

A thought transfixed me: for the first time in my life I saw the truth as it is set into song by so many poets, proclaimed as the final wisdom by so many thinkers. The truth—that love is the ultimate and the highest goal to which man can aspire. . . . I understood how a man who has nothing left in this world still may know bliss, be it only for a brief moment, in the contemplation of his beloved. In a position of utter desolation, when man cannot express himself in positive action, when his only achievement may consist in enduring his sufferings in the right way—an honorable way—in such a position man can, through loving contemplation of the image he carries of his beloved, achieve fulfillment. . . .

I did not know whether my wife was alive, and I had no means of finding out (during all my prison life there was no outgoing or incoming mail); but at that moment it ceased to matter. There was no need for me to know; nothing could touch the strength of my love, my thoughts, and the image of my beloved.

Sadly, Frankl's wife did not survive her confinement in a different concentration camp, which Frankl did not know until he was freed. But even though she had died, his wife—the thought of her—helped keep him alive. She was what mattered to him, the source of his meaning.

Old age can bring suffering, loss of hope, loss of faith in what a person has lived for. And while the challenges faced in aging rarely approach the intensity of those encountered in a concentration camp, we can experience a similar existential crisis that can be expressed in the single word *Why?* Why do I endure? What does it matter? What difference does my life make now?

Several people I interviewed spoke of this concern, even anxiety. As mentioned in the opening of part one, in most stages of our lives the tasks appropriate to that stage are laid out before us. But as we age, we may find fewer opportunities to participate in life's activities, fewer opportunities to make a difference. As Barbara P expressed it, "Suddenly I'm older. I'm taking up resources; I'm not contributing." Another person worried, "I'm just taking up space."

Bonnie K reflected on the difficulty of finding meaning or purpose at her stage of life. "I guess this purpose thing is really hard for me. It's hard for me to think about." When she was working, her life had focus. She knew what came next and when to do it. But for her, retirement coincided with moving to a new part of the country and a different living environment. "So I dealt with retirement and being here all at the same time, and I've been pretty lost as far as purpose goes." Previously, she said, "I had a core that was defining my existence. Now I feel like I'm spread so thin, so spread thin. I'm in churches, I'm in reading groups, I'm trying to make friends—that scattered kind of existence. It's much harder to feel like I have purpose. I have to do a lot more thinking and processing."

Meaning comes to us both by what is prescribed by the conditions of life in which we find ourselves and by the choices we make in response. Frankl emphasizes the power of choice each person possesses—the liberty to choose who we will be, no matter what our life's circumstances may be:

We who lived in concentration camps can remember the men who walked through the huts comforting others, giving away their last piece of bread. They may have been few in number, but they offer sufficient proof that everything can be taken from a man but one thing: the last of the human freedoms—to choose one's attitude in any given set of circumstances, to choose one's own way.

The power to decide who we will be is a factor in our lives at all stages, but it becomes especially important in our later years. Now, when the prescribed tasks of my life have been largely completed, what then matters to me? What meaning or meanings will I choose? Who will I be?

FIVE

Exemplars

I see a lot of quiet courage.
—Jack W, age 88

As we age, we look to those who have gone ahead to point the way along pathways we will likely follow. When we consider the question of meaning, others offer guidance. What do they have to tell us about who we can be in the later stages of life? Who do we admire? Who might we emulate? What possibilities does their example reveal? In my conversations with seniors, several cited people they regard as exemplars who serve as models for how they want to age.

JoWynn J spoke of one acquaintance who inspires her:

There's a woman who is 97. She just had her second hip replacement last month. She walks everywhere. She's having to use the walker now, but before the surgery last month, she was not using a walker. She was making pottery in the craft room. She belonged to the garden club, did flower arranging. She has traveled around the world; she's been to almost every part of the world taking videos. And then editing them herself. And then showing them in the auditorium. She's a vibrant, very active elderly woman who is in good spirits and very much contributing to the community. It would be great if I end up like her.

When I asked JoWynn to describe what it is about the woman that attracts her, she said, "It's continuing to participate in life and continuing to contribute." So meaning is created through participating in life, finding ways to stay involved and be engaged, even if in different ways than one has been accustomed to. Making adaptations so that it's possible to stay involved.

This theme was often cited by those I talked with. They looked to exemplars who modeled engagement with life, despite their age and limitations. One woman identified her mother and her aunt, "a tomboy, with a sense of humor, back in the 1890s." Both have been role models for her of how to be an active woman in each stage of life, including the later years.

And Catherine K, who is 83, spoke of her grandmother, who died at age 109 and who, when she was 104, made an appearance on the *Johnny Carson Show*. She said, "I think one of the contributions to her longevity was the fact that she was very involved with people. If she wasn't playing gin rummy or doing something with her friends, she was talking to them on the phone."

Tom B, who is 76, spoke of acquaintances older than he who are aging in a way that he hopes to emulate. These are people who have remained busy and productive as they have aged. Tom is retired from his career as a professional musician and professor. He remains active by continuing to perform, composing, writing, teaching, taking classes, and pursuing what he calls his "projects." "The one thing I can't stand," he confided, "is the notion of being bored. That would be the very worst thing."

As Tom looks ahead, he anticipates a time when he will not be able to maintain his current level of activity. Here, too, he looks to exemplars to show him how to live with limitations gracefully. "People," he explained, "who have approached the death and dying stage with as much good humor and objectivity as they could muster." He hopes to be such a person himself.

In his professional life, Jack W, who is 88, was a scientist and professor of physics at a major university. When first meeting him, Jack can come across as gruff and stern. I imagine him intimidating to a college undergraduate. But a conversation with him quickly reveals an active mind that has accumulated vast knowledge over a wide range of topics. When he retired from his professional career, he said, "There was a lot I wanted to learn about history and the social side of life and the artistic side of life. Things that I just never had time for." In retirement he was able to pursue these interests, such as by traveling and going to the theater. "I reveled in that. And I collected a lot of books on various subjects having nothing to do with science. That has been a great pleasure."

Dig a little deeper, and one finds a depth of human caring. For years, Jack volunteered to visit people in the assisted living section of his retirement community, offering his presence to those who were confined by their infirmities. "It's sympathy. It's attention," he said in describing his goals for these visits.

"I think that most people realize that there isn't much you can really do for them to improve their condition. But you can help them take their minds off themselves."

Jack has lived in this retirement community for fourteen years, having moved there with his wife when she began to show signs of dementia. As her condition worsened, she moved into assisted living. She and Jack did not have children to share responsibility for visiting and providing emotional support, so Jack took it upon himself. He was faithfully attentive to her during the period of her decline and death.

When I asked him about exemplars or models in dealing with the challenges of aging, he cited people who he encounters each day. "I see a lot of quiet courage here on the part of people who know they are in bad shape, who are trying to live through it. Something parallel to what I'm trying to do."

"What," I asked, "is 'quiet courage'?"

"Well," he said, "you don't go around complaining all the time, and you do what needs to be done, and you try to be civil and cheerful to people. It contrasts with some other people who become embittered and quarrelsome and complaining. And I think quiet courage looks like not giving way to emotion. It means being practical and trying to show a positive spirit. It means finding something good in each day."

Jack did not name himself as an exemplar of quiet courage, but I will. He spoke of his own declining health, brought on by age and also a condition characterized by an aggressive malfunctioning of the bone marrow, in which the production of red blood cells decreases. This illness is ultimately terminal, though a person can live with it for many years. In Jack's experience, it has meant increasing anemia and tiredness. It takes more effort to do anything.

When faced with such a condition, one may be tempted to withdraw. One pulls back from activities because they demand too much energy. But Jack has consciously resisted that temptation. He serves on committees in the retirement community, always attends meetings that keep residents informed of community governance issues, and has recently joined the League of Women Voters, both to support their work and to learn more about what they do. "I've always thought that I'm very deficient in knowledge of local politics," he said, a deficiency he hopes to address through his involvement in that organization. Jack keeps up with current events, seems to read the newspaper front to back each day, and also reads widely in areas of interest to him.

When I asked if there was anything else he has found important in living with his own aging, Jack named friendship. "It's really very important to have someone to talk to who is willing to talk on a more serious level." He admitted that forming friendships requires intentionality on his part, because, he said, "I'm not particularly gifted with the gift of gab." So he looks to those who share interests, who work with him on committees. "Learning to make new friends is a very important thing as you age, and it's hard. It's progressively harder, it seems to me, as you get older, to find the interests that can sustain a friendship."

One other quality I observed in Jack, which he didn't mention, is his lively sense of humor, which he inserts at times when one is not expecting it. To find humor in a situation that may be deadly serious is both a choice and also an expression of freedom. It's a refusal to be defeated by our afflictions. Laughter relieves life's heaviness, gives us the option of rising above what afflicts us.

Summing up his own sense of purpose that he calls upon to guide him through this period in his life, Jack advised, "Live day to day but try to contribute something, and try to socialize. And try to be realistic."

Susan H lives in the metropolitan Washington, D.C., area; Ken P is in Michigan. Susan is 72; Ken is 77. Both seek to age responsibly and well. And both identified people from whom they have learned—people who demonstrated how to approach challenges of the elder years. Susan named an aunt who never lost her sense of humanity as she faced the diminishments of age with honesty and gentleness. Ken spoke of his wife, Tawnya. Her way of facing terminal cancer made her his exemplar of how to live and die honorably.

Susan said,

> I had an aunt who never had children. She lived until she was close to 90, and she was always kind and patient. She was just a lovely, lovely woman, and when she couldn't do something, she would smile and say, "You know, I'm not as quick as I used to be. So just give me a few minutes." Like if we were at a restaurant or if we were getting in and out of a car. She would always do everything with such a gracious kindness to her that your heart opened up, and you just wanted to do all you could for her. I had such respect for her, and she never lost her sense of humanity or caring about others. Yes, I would say she was my number one person I would look up to.

Her aunt's graciousness and humanity was part of her appeal for Susan. But so was her honesty. She didn't hesitate to ask when she needed help. "She said what she needed, and that was very helpful. It was a way to relate to her. Instead of pretending or shoving it aside, she might say, 'Give me a hand. Here, would you carry this? It's heavy.' Whatever. She would state what she needed in the nicest way."

Ken spoke with admiration of Tawnya's response to her diagnosis of ovarian cancer. She lived for a year after diagnosis, and the example she set has given him a model for how to withstand the extreme duress of an illness that not only is terminal but also causes considerable suffering. He remarked particularly about her honesty in facing the cancer.

As a parish minister, Ken has seen many people afflicted with a terminal illness. Sometimes, he observed, both those who have cancer and their families avoid talking about it. No one speaks about what everyone knows is happening. They continue with their lives as if these were ordinary days. So there is no way to acknowledge the stresses all are living with, no way to say goodbye, no way to bring this person's life story to completion. When the inevitable death occurs, the survivors are left with words unsaid, thoughts unexpressed, and lingering regrets.

By contrast, Tawnya was open about her illness and honest about how it was going to end. Ken remembered the day of the surgery, when doctors made a last-ditch effort to arrest the cancer. But it had spread; there was nothing the doctors could do. "I knew," Ken said, "that she was going to die very soon. I got to her hospital room and was waiting for her. When she came, and they had gotten her placed in the bed, she said, 'You don't have to be falsely cheerful. I heard what they said. I'm going to die.' And I said, 'Whoa. I was supposed to be the one to tell you that.' She said, 'I know, but you know me. I'm always overhearing something.' And we spent the afternoon talking. Her honesty, her frankness, were quite remarkable."

Arrangements were made for her to be admitted into hospice care. "And, you know, one of the first things she said when she got there was, 'I need to talk to someone about what's going to happen to my body when I die.'" Once that was accomplished, "she proceeded to have what she called 'one of the best weeks of my life.'" Family and friends came to see her, including her oldest high school friend, who traveled from Ohio. Her parents arrived, as did her brothers. "She was having, she said, 'the time of my life!' She said, 'It's a real shame you have to die in order to have so much fun!'

"She told her grandchildren, 'I want you to watch me. I want you to see how to die.' And they still remember that." For himself, Ken said, her openness meant that he didn't have to hide anything. He didn't have to perform that complicated dance—so familiar to those around the dying—of maneuvering around what to say, what not to say. "It meant I could share completely openly with her."

I suggested that even as Tawnya was dying, she was helping people. She was showing the way for them. It was not a meaningless death.

Ken agreed. "That's the kind of person she was, Bruce. Three days before she died, she went online." He paused, laughing. "She went online and ordered six shirts from L. L. Bean, thinking I was running low on shirts!" He laughed again. "I said, 'Tawnya, for heaven's sake!' She said, 'Oh, I know how many shirts you have. I know more than you do.' Well, it may be true, OK. But that kind of spirit, yeah."

Andrea N is 69 years old, newly retired from her career as a museum curator for the Smithsonian Institution. She lives alone, her family is small and scattered throughout the country. She is attentive to the challenges of aging; she wants to be prepared for whatever occurs.

She has worked out the physical and financial arrangements that will support her through the years ahead. This has involved moving to a new apartment, consulting with a financial advisor, staying in touch with family, and maintaining a network of friends and acquaintances. Andrea has managed the transition out of her professional career by "downsizing" it. She continues to teach part-time on a schedule that has been gradually shrinking. She has also found ways to use the expertise she has developed in other realms, serving on one committee promoting art in the community where she lives and on another involved with African-American history.

She approaches her senior years realistically. At a stage in life when many are still denying they will ever get old, she looks at aging straight on. "Time marches on," Andrea says. "Stuff happens to you, and you don't know what's gonna happen. I'm not wishing for it; nobody wishes for it. You get older; stuff does happen."

For inspiration and guidance, she looks to those who are older than she is and confront a variety of health concerns, those who have experienced losses far greater than she has and refuse to be weighed down by them. "Nothing seems to stop them," she observes. "It would be easy for them to feel sorry for themselves, stay off by themselves, but they don't do that. They come out! They interact with people. They say, 'No, I'm not going to define myself by my infirmities. I'm a person. I'll give as much as I can.'"

"I find that inspiring," Andrea says. It is inspiring to encounter those who are elderly and who have experienced

many losses yet are still determined to "let people know that
I'm here!"

Her advice to those who are entering their own senior
years: "Take it light, take it easy, enjoy the moments that you
have. Don't project so far out into the future that you forget
to enjoy yourself and the people around you. And be glad for
everything you've got, be glad for the people you've got. Do the
best that you can."

In the retirement community where I serve as chaplain, I
sometimes encounter a woman taking a walk through the halls.
She is immaculately dressed, her clothes colorful and graceful;
she looks physically fit, her hair is styled, she wears makeup
tastefully applied, she smiles and greets each person who passes
by, projecting a sense of elegance. She has one leg.

She walks with crutches carefully placed to support her as
she makes her way, slowly but resolutely. I do not know this
woman's name. I have never talked with her, except to exchange
pleasantries in passing. But to me she is a visible representation
of courage in the face of loss. It cannot be easy to take that
walk, making her way on one leg and two crutches, supporting
herself with the muscles in her arms. She must spend considerable time getting ready: choosing clothes, applying makeup,
making sure that her hair is ready to be seen. It must take emotional energy to present herself to the world, offering smiles
of welcome to those she passes. There must be days when she
doesn't want to do it.

And yet, she bears that witness to life. When she smiles and
greets those she encounters, they almost always smile and greet
her in return. In so doing, she creates energy that enlivens her
and those with whom she comes into contact. I see her as an
example of, to use Jack W's terminology, "quiet courage." And

as someone who, in Andrea N's words, has decided, "I'm not going to define myself by my infirmities. I'm a person."

In seeking meaning during our final years, we look to other people to serve as guides, advisors, allies. What matters to them? How does the meaning they find affect the quality of their lives? How have they managed the transitions of age, and what do they call upon to help show the way? Who do we admire, and what of their example can we incorporate for ourselves?

Themes emerge in response to these questions. We see people continuing to participate in life, despite the adaptations they must make. We find people who remain productive—making contributions—even if not at the level of previous years. We see those who remain engaged with other people, taking the risk of making new friendships even as they have lost friends. Some find meaning by continuing to offer service, by caring, by taking up a project that helps someone else. We look at how others live during these years and find that honesty is a trait much valued, as is courage in the face of honesty. There are people who inspire us by the grace with which they confront the challenges before them and those who treat others kindly even as they themselves are under stress. We also find those who steadfastly retain their integrity, refusing to let themselves be defined by the circumstances of their lives.

Each of these traits is noteworthy. Each can reveal a vital source of meaning. But even more important than any of these specific qualities is an underlying message conveyed by how they live. That message is that we have the power to choose who we will be, despite the vicissitudes of fate such as illness, accident, the genetic pool that defines our vulnerabilities, social class, and the economic resources available to us. All have their

effects, but we retain the ultimate power and freedom to determine our character, to choose the messages we wish to convey
—the affirmations we make—by how we conduct our lives.

When Viktor Frankl's book was published in English, it was
given the title *Man's Search for Meaning*. But the original title,
translated from the German, meant "Saying Yes to Life in Spite
of Everything." Saying *Yes* to life underscores the role of choice,
"in spite of everything" that might happen to us. We can make
choices that affirm life, just as we also have the power to say no.
Withdrawal is a choice. Despair is a choice. As are avoidance,
orneriness, pessimism, and giving up. All are choices.

We also choose our role models, those who demonstrate
through their living how we want to live and who we seek to
be. We look to those who point the way toward participating
in life to the fullest extent available to us: to engaging, treating
others with kindness and respect, showing compassion, living
with courage—in spite of everything that makes these difficult
to do. We look to those who bear witness to the possibility of
saying *Yes* and for examples of how we might incorporate this
choice into our own living.

1.

Are there people you regard as exemplars who guide you in
how to age? What attracts you to them?

2.

Can you identify people who have shown you, by their example, how you do *not* want to age? How would you choose to age
differently from them?

3.

Are you aware of being a model for others as you age? What do you want others to know about aging and how to address its challenges?

4.

What core values and qualities are most important for you to honor as you make your way through the later stages of your life?

SIX

Choice

You've got to find meaning for yourself.
That's what it comes down to. That's the safety net.
—Barbara L, age 75

As we age, "stuff happens," in Andrea N's words. Our bodies break down in different ways and in different sequences. One person has heart problems; another is subject to diabetes; another struggles with memory loss; another contracts cancer; another experiences a series of small strokes. More often than not, several of these conditions interact with each other.

Circumstances also shift. For some people, retirement savings provide more than adequate income for their senior years. Others find balancing income with expenditures to be a constant challenge. Some people have attentive family members who are always available to them. Others struggle with isolation and loneliness. Some live in an environment offering opportunities for learning, involvement, and community.

Others find that their opportunities for pursuing interests and relationship diminish, and they get terribly bored.

Yet, despite the challenges we encounter—the "stuff" that happens—we still have choice. We possess the power to choose how we will respond to both the hardships and the opportunities, how we will live during our later years. Just as we have the power to influence who we will seek to be. Viktor Frankl, writing of his experience in the concentration camp, observed, "The sort of person the prisoner became was the result of an inner decision." That's true of aging too: the sort of person we become at this stage of life results from the choices we make.

Groucho Marx put it this way: "I, not events, have the power to make me happy or unhappy today. I can choose which it shall be. Yesterday is dead, tomorrow hasn't arrived yet. I have just one day, today, and I'm going to be happy in it."

Ruth W was well into her 80s when I was a young man serving as minister of her church on Long Island. She told wonderful stories about her past, such as of the friendship her family shared with that of Jack Kerouac, the beat writer. She sighed and remembered, "He had such deep, *deep* blue eyes."

Ruth helped me out when I was just starting at that church. At the time, I was 33 years old, a generation or two younger than much of the congregation. Some considered me too young to understand the conditions of their lives, too young to be their minister. But Ruth shut down the grumbling with a gentle observation. "I believe Jesus was 33, wasn't he?"

Ruth was a person you could talk to with complete confidence that she would listen and appreciate. She would try to understand you, where you were coming from, and would not issue a judgment unless you asked for her advice. As a result, she was beloved by people from diverse walks of life, including the LGBTQ community, which was just then beginning to come out. She was invited to parties where she might have been about the only straight person there: an old lady with people gathered around her.

I asked her, "Have you always been this way, with such connections to people?" I expected her to say "yes," with appropriate humility—or maybe she wouldn't know what I was talking about.

But her response surprised me: "No, I have not always been this way." She continued, "My husband had died. I was living alone in a little house. Nobody visited me. I was feeling sorry for myself. I was becoming resentful. And then I thought, 'Well, I'm not doing anything for anybody else, either.' So I decided to change."

She made a choice to draw upon a different part of herself, not the lonely and resentful side but the part of her that knew how to enjoy other people and support them. That choice made the difference.

It is a phenomenon well known to those in contact with the elderly: some try very hard to make connections and maintain relationships, no matter what obstacles they confront. Others seal themselves behind closed doors. They rarely see or are seen by anybody else. A social worker in a retirement community, observed, "You can put two 90-year-olds together—both with the same diagnosis. One may say, 'Well, this is one more challenge I've got to get through.' The other concludes, 'This is the beginning of the end.' Their paths may be the same medically, but how they respond to it and what it means to them is different." Pat K, who is 73, observed that "there's a wide gamut in how people age. Some succumb to the aging process. Then

there are others who are in their 90s and even early 100s who
are still going full steam ahead."

Why the difference? Why do some people rise to the challenges that present themselves as they age, and why do others
give up?

To some degree, responses are guided by one's tempera-
ment, which is set very early in life. Some people approach
the world with a positive outlook that persists no matter what
obstacles appear. Others are more prone to worry, anxiety,
expecting the worst from even a good situation.

But it's not all predetermined. Those I talked with consistently identified another influence: attitude. A professional
who works with the elderly offered her observation of what dis-
tinguishes those who age well from those who do not: "I really
think it's about attitude, which you can do something about."
Yes, "stuff happens." But then we claim the right to determine
what we will do in response to stuff.

"I think the more resilient we are," Barbara L said, "the
better we handle these challenges that life confronts us with."

I asked her to elaborate: "Do you see resilience as a quality that is innate, or do we have the power to become more
resilient?"

"It's a choice," she responded. "The more willing a person
is to think, 'OK, this hurts—whatever has happened—this is
hard, this is really, really hard. What do I need to do here to
take care of myself?' And I'm not talking a five-year plan; I'm
talking one step. 'What's one step I can take right now to help
me deal with this?' The more one-steps we can take, then the
steps get bigger, and we can do more."

Pat K spoke of her arthritis and how it could limit her
activity. And yet she pushes herself to take on projects that she

wants to do, despite the discomfort she experiences. As a result, she has stayed more active than might be expected. "I shouldn't be able to quilt with the grip that I have, but I've made four quilts for my grandchildren, and I'm determined to keep doing those kinds of things."

Lowell S spoke of a woman who exhibited a positive and resourceful attitude in approaching the physical conditions to which she was subject. She suffered from sickle cell anemia and debilitating arthritis, was confined to a wheelchair, lived in a studio apartment. Lowell said,

> I saw her one day in a store; she lived right near me. We had a nice "Hello, hello." Then I ran into her in several other stores, including a grocery store that's close to us. She was in one of the power chairs and had an aide to help her. She was totally peppy. I said, "I won't see you for a while because I'm going to be away." She said, "Oh, well, have a nice vacation."
>
> I came back and the next time I saw her, which was close to two weeks later, I knocked on her door and she said, "Oh, I'm glad you're back. Did you have a nice vacation?" I said to her, "Boy, you've got a memory like a bear trap." I've never forgotten her answer; she said, "There's nothing wrong with my mind, it's my body that doesn't work."

By contrast, Lowell offered the example of a man who wore an NSA (National Security Agency) T-shirt to whom he delivered Meals on Wheels. "I tried to engage him in conversation for a year and a half and never got more out of him than 'Thank you for coming by.' Nothing. He would not engage. I tried him with current issues; I tried him with his cat; I tried him with his T-shirt—anything to get him going, but he wouldn't engage." In Lowell's experience, men have a harder time making positive adjustments to aging than women. He speculated that perhaps it is because women are more proficient at forming relationships with each other, while men are more likely to be competitive.

Lucille K identified the importance of taking action to stay engaged with life. "You have to use initiative. You can't wait for somebody to come knocking on your door and say, 'Hey, would you like to do this?' You've got to make things work for yourself." Mildred H also identified the role of choice in determining the direction to move in life. "You have choices in life. You can opt for being a really vile person. You can opt for being a very ordinary person." Or you can choose steps that help build an attitude of resilience, of openness, of reaching out to others, of seeking possibility. And Rita D observed that while she does have a tendency to see the bright side, she also makes choices that enhance her natural inclinations. "I see the good in things," she said. But also, "I *look* for the good."

As people age, some become more focused on themselves. They appear to lose interest in others and in the outside world. Yet there are also those who remain active, nourishing relationships and continuing to learn. Susan H commented, "The real occupational hazard of being a senior is a tendency to close down, to shut down and let your life get narrower and narrower. It's a refusal to accept that this is another stage of life. It's not death. It's a stage of life. You want to live until you die, right? You have to not shut that door and shut down and watch TV because your life will very rapidly close in on you."

Identify an interest, she advised, and develop it. She offered an example drawn from her own life: "Even if it's only taking care of wild birds in the winter. Get out there and feed them and find that you know nothing about birds. So you get a bird guide and take some notes, and then when your grandchildren come, you can tell them what kind of bird that is. Every opportunity that you have to live, grab it!"

The attitude these seniors identified is not a perpetual optimism that expects everything will turn out for the best. It also need not be a belief that all things happen for good reasons, even if you cannot see them in the present moment. This attitude, rather, involves deciding what you need to do in order to address the problems and the challenges that confront you. It's the determination to look realistically at the available options and go with those that support the life you choose as yours.

Stephen C, who is 77, noted that articles and books available for those anticipating the transition from the world of work to retirement tend to focus on money. That is, will you have enough money to retire? But just as important—probably more so—is another question: "Who are you going to be?" The choices we make in response to that question set the course we will follow in our later years.

Along with attitude, many seniors cite realism as a factor that guides them through the choices they make. They look squarely at what they are facing, assess the range of possible options and likely outcomes, and then they take action. Susan H spoke of the need to plan for one's own aging. She said, "You have to do preparation for it. Just as we had prepared before marriage and children: we thought about what kind of marriage we would like, and we planned for being parents. I think when you're aging, you start reading about what to expect, what to anticipate, and how to best prepare for it."

She concluded, "It's important to prepare to get old. Okay, I'm not going to get out of this." What can we do to address what we are likely to encounter in the months and years ahead?

Bette H cited realism in thinking about life conditions that are likely to change in one's life:

> Men need to know how to cook if the wife is disabled and vice versa. If one person is doing bills and then suddenly that person can't pay the bills, the other person needs to know how. You need to know how you keep the papers for the taxes. I've heard about people where the husband is taking care of the finances. And then he gets a little bit of dementia, and he's trading in stocks and suddenly, all the money's gone, and she doesn't know anything about what he's been doing.
>
> You need to know which handymen to call, for example: who fixes the furnace. Also, both husband and wife need to know how to shop for groceries. We discovered that one when I couldn't go shopping. My husband didn't know how to get what I usually buy. I mean, he didn't have a clue!

Some of the choices we need to make as we grow older seem obvious, even though they might represent a considerable loss. Martha C reported that, at age 90, she finally put away her roller skates for good. But she glowed at memories of gliding around the rink, particularly when she and her partner were in sync, effortlessly sensing each other's moves.

Gail T noted that when she and her husband moved to a new home, they were careful to locate themselves on a bus route, anticipating a time when neither of them would be able to drive. Some spoke of making housing choices that take into account possible future disabilities, such as by avoiding homes with stairs even if, at present, they were quite mobile. Others spoke of the need for realism in finances, while several people cited realism in the realm of medical treatments. Lucille K, who is 87, said, "I've already told the doctor that I'm not going to take certain tests anymore because I don't believe I would be willing to go through what it takes to get through the treatment. Cancer, in particular. I have two sisters who died from cancer, and after all that they went through, they died anyway. I think that if medicine hadn't gotten as far as it has, people would die when they're supposed to rather than just trying to prolong life without making it better. What's the good of spending two or three years doing that?"

When specific disabilities begin to appear, we have choices. One strategy is to ignore them, conduct our lives as if nothing has changed. It is a strategy, but not one likely to be successful, at least not for very long. Something will happen—it's almost guaranteed. Something will happen that announces we can't live as we once did.

A better way is to make accommodations along the way that enable us to maintain our lives. JoWynn J spoke of her mother, who had dementia. Sometimes she would forget having had a visitor. Rather than denying her memory lapse, and rather than dismissing it as an aberration, she worked out a plan to address future such occurrences. She acquired a guest book and asked her visitors to write down their name and the date when they visited. Then, the next day, she could check her book as a reminder of who had been there.

JoWynn's mother also made accommodations by writing notes to herself. "She had notes all over her apartment as her memory declined and deteriorated. She tried hard to hold onto her mind; she really worked at it. She was not in denial; she was accepting of what was happening to her, even while she tried to remain as independent as possible."

JoWynn remembered, "One day I was walking down the hall with her, and a woman approached us and asked how to get to the fitness center. My mother told her and as we walked away from that woman, she said, 'She asks me that question every day.' Then my mother said, 'I'm not the only one losing my mind.' And I said, 'Mother, does it concern you that you're losing your mind?' And she said, 'No, I just take it as it comes.'"

This strikes me as a practical response. It combines realism—that is, being mindful of what is actually occurring—with attitude: the decision to live on our own terms, despite the challenges that get hurled our way.

What about bad choices? If we support the right of seniors to make their own decisions, might they pursue options that turn out to be unwise? Isn't it our duty to be caring and responsible, to guide them toward choices that will enhance their lives and protect them from the trouble they can get themselves into?

There are times when an elderly person becomes a danger to self and society. Some should not be driving. Some should not have unfettered access to their finances. Some should not use a cooktop with an open flame. Some are unable to keep track of their medications. Some forget to eat. Some should not keep a loaded gun in their home. Some get lost when they venture away from familiar environs. But this isn't much different from those at any age who become unable to live safely. In these cases, intervention is necessary to protect people from themselves and to protect others.

Other choices, though, do not immediately threaten anything except, perhaps, our own ideas of how our loved one should live. If we are too quick to intervene—too quick to assert our own power and judgment over those of the senior— we may undermine that person's self-worth and weaken their ability to live their own life. More may be at stake than the particular choice in front of us.

A social worker at a retirement community remembered, "We had a resident move in who had diabetes and was never good at managing it herself. She didn't want to take the medicine, didn't care about her diet, didn't check her blood pressure as she should. But this had always been her history. It's just the way she's been. The family thought that we were going to fix her diabetes. That we were going to manage it for her."

But the role of the professional is not to take over another person's life. The same goes for the elderly person's family— their role is not to make sure their loved one follows all the rules. As long as a person understands the potential consequences of their decisions, they should be free to make what we may consider the wrong choices. The role of professional and family alike is to listen, be respectful of the senior's wishes, and then, perhaps, get out of the way.

It is often remarked that at a certain point in life, the roles of parent and child reverse. While the parent once took care of the child, now the adult child takes care of the elderly parent. And while the parent once monitored the actions of a child, guiding the child's choices toward what is right and true and healthy, now the adult child takes on the same role with Mom or Dad.

But the child-to-parent/parent-to-child analogy is flawed. Our parents will always be our parents, no matter what degree of assistance they need to negotiate the world. To treat them as children can be profoundly demeaning. It also renders them less able to function on their own. Once we turn over decision making to others—even a loved one who has our "best interests" at heart—we lose confidence in our own abilities. We lose our center and then we do, in fact, start to assume the role of a child.

A social worker I interviewed put it this way: "I will fight for someone's right to make the bad decision. It's kind of like freedom of speech, you know. I disagree with you, but I'll fight to the end to allow you to have the freedom to say it." She added, "I think that's really tough for families."

It is also quite possible that we may be wrong in our assumptions about what is right for a senior. My father is a happy and healthy 96-year-old whose mind is sharp and active. Throughout his life, he has never exercised in a systematic way, he has always struggled with his weight, and in his diet he has shown a preference for ice cream and pastries. He has kept visits to doctors to a minimum. My wife and I, well, we are of the "crunchy granola" generation. We have been careful about what we eat, believing that proper diet is a route to good health, both physical and spiritual. We have chosen whole grains, stayed away from saturated fats and the dreaded trans fats, limited our meat consumption, shunned fast food, worn sun block, exercised, maintained enviable BMIs (body mass indexes), kept regular doctor's appointments—and we have both endured bouts with cancer. My wife was diagnosed in her mid-50s, I in my early 60s. My father has faced no serious threats to his health. He still goes to work every day, he lives in his own house, he can drive—legally—without glasses. (Since the day I received my license at age 16, I have never been able to drive without glasses;

life is not fair.) I have no right to impose my "sensible" choices on my father because there's a good probability they would not be sensible for him.

In the retirement community where I serve as a chaplain, the vast majority of people are happy to be there. I know that because I ask, "Are you happy here? Are you glad that you moved into this community?" Most say, "Yes!" Quite a few of those are enthusiastic; some express regret that they hadn't made the decision to move earlier.

But there are exceptions. Some people are quite discontented, and they resent being there. The reason usually has little to do with the facility itself. It is, rather, that they feel they were forced to make the move—sometimes by circumstances or by their families. Perhaps the adult children decided that Mom or Dad or both would be better off in a community that offered medical care, regular meals, activities, community, and a safe environment. Or perhaps they realized that, despite their heartfelt desire and best efforts, they were simply unable to provide their parent with the care the older person needed. Moving into a retirement community can be sensible or even necessary, but it may not be welcomed when the move is made without the consent of the person moved. Joyce T observed, "On rare occasions, you run into somebody whose daughter or son has placed them here. They didn't make the decision, and they are not happy."

What matters, then, is not the power to make the *right* choice. It's the power to make choices, good ones and bad ones, everyday ones as well as those that may have far-reaching consequences. It's the power to make mistakes rather than being protected from them. For in that power of choice, we retain our humanity. As we age, our sense of personhood seems at risk as we lose the power to participate in what have been normal everyday activities. With choice, we assert our power to stay involved. We claim our right to be human beings.

Wini W had been an activist throughout her life. The daughter of an American Baptist minister and his wife, she grew up with an understanding of Christianity that emphasized social justice and working for peace. The name her parents chose for her, "Winifred," means "maker of peace," a destiny that Wini took seriously.

As a young woman, she settled with her husband in a community of like-minded people in Vermont, where they sought to live in harmony with the natural surroundings while also witnessing for justice. They secured a small plot of land, built their own home, and began raising a family that eventually included five children. Wini and her husband grew their own food, cooked on an open fire or a woodstove, canned their produce, made their own bread, churned butter, made cheese.

Wini viewed herself first and foremost as a citizen of the world. She committed herself to promoting social justice wherever she lived throughout the years. She taught in a one-room schoolhouse, was a social worker for the school system, and worked for the Head Start program in West Virginia. She organized resistance to the civil defense program created during the Cold War; she worked with a group opposed to uranium mining in their community when she lived in Virginia; she monitored police activity to ensure that the police followed the law; she participated in many demonstrations and organizations promoting peace and environmental awareness. And Wini continued her activism when she and her husband moved into a retirement community, founding an organization called

Seekers of Justice in which participants stayed current on social justice concerns.

When she reached her 90s, Wini descended deeply into dementia. She always recognized her children, but when I visited her, she did not speak, and I wasn't sure she knew who I was. But she set her gaze on me, and she held my hand tightly.

Then I heard that she was refusing food and water. When the staff tried to feed her, she closed her mouth tight, shook her head, and would not let herself be force fed. As a result, she died after several days. Her children understood immediately. As one of them put it, "Damn! She did it!" Despite being in the throes of dementia, Wini reached into what was left of her capacity and made a choice. She chose to exert control—to claim the terms of her own life. It was her last expression of the idealism to which she had devoted her life.

1.

What choices have you made in response to your aging? What difference have these choices made?

2.

Some people remain active as they age. Others withdraw. How do you account for the difference?

3.

Barbara L advised that when confronted with the challenges of aging, we ask ourselves, "What's one step I can take right now to help me deal with this?" Can you think of one step that you could take today to address a concern or an issue you have been struggling with?

4.

What is your preference: to make sure that "good" decisions are made for you, even if that means turning your decision making over to others? Or to retain the authority to make decisions for yourself, even if you might sometimes make "bad" ones? Why?

SEVEN

Relationship

It's important to make friends.
But it's harder to do when you're old
than when you're young.
—Susan H, age 72

A snowstorm closed all the schools on a winter day in How-
ard County, Maryland. The county government offices and
services were also shut down, including the senior center. But
people still showed up at the senior center, despite the snow
and notices that it would be closed. They came even though
travel was challenging and the footing on icy pathways was
treacherous. It's a testament not only to the tenacity of seniors
but also to the importance of the relationships we form. Relationships matter throughout our lives. Among the elderly, they
become a crucial source of meaning and well-being.

The events of that snowy day were reported by Lowell S,
a volunteer at the Florence Bain Senior Center in Columbia,

Maryland. Lowell, who is in his mid-70s, is a journalist by profession. He facilitates a weekly discussion group focused on current events. "The beauty of current events," he said, "is that it's new every week. The slowest week of the year always has new stuff in it that you can talk about." The group helps participants stay current about what's happening in the nation and in the world. But Lowell understands that another purpose is to help create and nourish social relationships. Participants have the opportunity to get to know each other, start conversations that extend beyond these sessions, and build friendships. It helps them address a primary challenge of aging: the diminishing number of relationships available to us as we grow older.

A loss of relationships often goes hand in hand with aging and with declining health. A survey of 148 studies on the relationship between health and social relationships, discussed on the University of Minnesota's *Taking Charge of Your Health and Wellbeing* website (www.takingcharge.csh.umn.edu), found a 50 percent higher rate of death among those without friends, compared with those who had a strong social network. The only other lifestyle factor with such a significant effect was smoking; the death rate of smokers and the death rate of those without friends were about the same. Other risk factors, such as obesity, high cholesterol, alcohol abuse, and high blood pressure, were not as dangerous to one's health as lack of friendships. Another study concluded that men in their 50s who would seem to be at high risk because of their very low social and economic status, but who have a lot of friends, live considerably longer than men with high status but few friends. Our lives depend on our relationships. Not just the quality of our lives, but life itself.

Many people are lonely in their final years. As Lowell S put it, "When you get older, you look around, and people are dying off or moving away." The social contacts that have sustained us decrease. Not only do old friends and family members die, there are fewer opportunities to make new friends. It's also harder to participate in everyday conversation with acquaintances and strangers. We become less mobile and are not able to get to places where we can be around other people. Our health declines, and we might not have the energy it takes to maintain relationships. Among the very elderly who are institutionalized, friends and family gradually cut back on their visits, or they stop coming altogether. This occurs not just with younger family members but with contemporaries, those who used to be friends. They stop visiting because it's too hard to see their friend failing. As a result, the elderly become isolated, which often leads to depression. Isolation and depression can be significant problems as we age.

Sometimes, too, when our lives become less busy during the retirement years, we recognize a need for human contact that might always have been with us but that we haven't taken the time to acknowledge. When we are younger, our lives are filled with tasks and responsibilities: raising children, doing our jobs, taking care of houses and cars and the chores that accompany everyday life. We might not have time to acknowledge an unfulfilled yearning for closer human contact.

Barbara L said, "You don't have the work and just the busyness of life to mask loneliness. The loneliness that I think is part of the human condition comes glaring out when you're older because so much of our other stuff is stripped away. I've talked to my friends about it, even my guy friends—my two guy friends. One's a widower, an unexpected widower; it very quickly happened. And the other is married: a happy marriage. They said, 'Boy, loneliness is tough. We never expected it.'"

The need for relationships during the senior years came up in many of the conversations I had. People spoke about how difficult it was to make new friends and keep them as they grew older. Jack W emphasized the importance of making new friends but noted that it has become progressively harder for him to find people with the shared interests necessary to sustain a friendship. Among his contemporaries he finds a narrowing of interests—and then the opportunities for contact and meaningful conversation also decrease. He said, "I guess I had thought that physically it would decline but intellectually it would remain active, but I don't believe that's always true." With the narrowing that may accompany aging, there just isn't enough to talk about to keep people engaged. He also finds a tendency among his contemporaries to repeat stories about themselves, endlessly, usually drawn from their young adult years. When a person lives in the past, there is little room for relationship in the present.

Jack's belief in maintaining a wide range of interests as a basis for friendship was echoed by several other people I spoke with. Staying engaged with issues in the world gave them a means for establishing relationships; it also sustained them during difficult times. Joyce T spoke of her husband's death as the most significant loss of her life. But, she said, she received support and strength as a result of relationships she had developed through her various commitments and from having a wider range of concerns to claim her attention. Her commitment to human rights gave her ideals to strive for—beyond herself—even when she had experienced deep personal loss.

Susan H noted the value of having people to talk to about aging itself and how aging is affecting one's life: "It's important to discuss it. It's important to make friends. But it's harder to do when you're old than when you're young. Since I moved here across the country, I truly had to make a concerted effort to find some girlfriends. Fortunately, I've met some lovely, lovely women, and that's an important part of my life."

She spoke of taking advantage of technology, saying, "You know, because of the Internet, we're able to connect. I'm able to talk to my father's sister, who is almost as old as my mother. She lives in Los Angeles, and we talk at least three times a week, by email or playing Words with Friends. How wonderful is that? I've got her in my life because of the abilities created by the electronic age."

Her mother, Susan said, had shunned computers. She wouldn't consider the possibility of learning what they could do for her. "Too bad. It isolated her even more. That was a chance to open her world." By contrast, Susan's aunt is housebound, but she maintains contact with friends and relatives throughout the country. I am reminded of my daughter-in-law's grandmother, who lives in a small city in India, in the foothills of the Himalayas. Yet she interacts with people throughout the world through social media. She has her "Facebook time" each day. And she always comments on the photos that her Facebook friends post.

Friendships developed during the later stages of life are often different from those that come earlier. "They're not as deep," one person said. Another noted that "it can take years" to establish a meaningful friendship. Relationships established among the elderly don't have as much time to develop. A woman spoke of new friends she has made through living in a retirement community, but she noted that her relationships with them lack the depth of those developed earlier. "I count them as my friends," she observed, "but that doesn't mean I know a lot about them."

It is not clear to me whether relationships begun later in life remain superficial because of a lack of time and opportunity to develop them or because the participants prefer them that way. Seniors often can be hesitant to commit to new relationships. When you have lost friends through illness or death, you may become reluctant to start again with someone new. Barbara P expressed it succinctly: "The fact that people die all the time is tough." Or, as another put it, "Everybody's dying who is our age." And Rita D observed, "Sometimes I think, 'Don't get too close to people.' You may die or they may die." She has lost some "very nice lady friends" over the years, but "you get over it. It's part of the process, you know."

Yet some seniors I talked with have found ways around the difficulties inherent in making friends and finding support during the later senior years.

Ron B is an African-American man living in a retirement community in which he is in a distinct minority: the population is mostly white women. His own wife has dementia and requires constant care from him. He needs support and friendship—a break from the stresses of caring for his wife. There are only two other African-American men in that community, and one has dementia. He has had to reach beyond those who would normally be in the pool of those available to him for friendship.

Kate L told me about her mother making a connection with a person with whom she might not have normally interacted. But the shared experience of aging, itself, broke down barriers. She said,

> My mother really was Russian—Russian Jewish. She was sitting on a bench with an African-American woman.

She would call her "a black." As I'm walking up to them, my mother was saying, "Never mind. There's good and bad in all kinds." And I thought how condescending that sounded. (I was—I am—a real knee-jerk liberal. And I hope to die that way. Jerking my knees for good causes!) I thought, I'm going to die to listen to that. So I come up closer and the African-American woman is turning to my mother and says, "Ain't that the truth!" and they went on to talk about the good and bad in each of their lives, of people in their lives. And they were saying the same thing, and they understood each other. They were two old ladies sitting on a park bench and talking about the world they lived in and had always lived in, and they understood.

When Frances R was in her early 80s, she met Michael W, who was in his late 80s. Both were widowed, both had retired years earlier from their respective professions—Frances as a social worker, Michael a college professor. They shared interests, they enjoyed each other's company, they became friends, and soon they had formed a relationship. They became a committed couple. "We both know this will end badly," she told me. That is, one or the other of them will get sick; one will die before the other in a relatively short time, leaving their partner behind. In that sense, the relationship was doomed.

They had been faced with a decision: whether to expose themselves to the pain of a relationship that would end before it had time to fully develop or take the chance of seeing where this new relationship would take them.

In the end, love won out. They decided that this was a gift to them: an unexpected gift as they both neared the end of life.

They chose to accept it, despite the risk of loss that their relationship exposed them to. The last time I saw them—before I moved
away from their community—was at an art exhibit. They were
holding hands, moving from painting to painting. They were
absorbed in the art and in each other. I don't think they noticed
I was there, which is as it should be when love is young.

John G is 82; Gail T is 76. They consider themselves to be
newlyweds as they approach their third anniversary. Gail was
widowed twice before entering into this, her third marriage;
John's wife died five years ago. Gail had also experienced the
death of her son the year before. They were not strangers to loss.

Before becoming a couple, they had been friends for many
years, as had their spouses. John and Gail worked together on
church committees. They saw each other frequently through
the everyday life of the congregation. Gail remembered, "And
then, for some strange reason—you know, these things do
happen—our relationship began to change. It is *never* too late
for romance. Absolutely! Trust it! You may think that a part of
your former life, but I'm here to tell you: not so!" John added,
"We both looked at ourselves and said, 'Why are we wasting
the rest of our lives lying around? Let's get together and make
something happen!'"

In some ways, romance is the same no matter your age.
But the sense of purpose is different in our later years. John
and Gail had spent their earlier married years attending to
the essential tasks of living: creating a home, raising children,
pursuing careers, becoming financially stable—John spent
his working years in government service, while Gail developed
her own business. Now, in retirement, their concerns have
shifted. They are devoting time, attention, and resources to
creating a legacy.

They are bringing their life experience to church committee work, helping revise and clarify practices of church governance and extending the programming available within their congregation. They both oversee small scholarship programs, which they have set up to help those of younger generations. And they are deeply involved with their families, offering assistance now to help provide for the future.

They want to pass on something of what they have learned in their long, good lives. Gail said,

> I have made a point with my grandchildren that I want them to understand that life does not stop as long as you're still living. It goes on. You have funny things happen to you, and you have wonderful things happen to you, and surprises and new adventures, and you have to keep reaching for those.
>
> You will have disappointments, of course, and heartaches. But if they don't know now how to recover from that, then they will never have the nerve to take a risk. And I think it's by taking risks that we move forward.

Joyce N was also widowed twice. Her first husband died when she was 43. Her second husband died when she was in her 60s. At that point, she "just about decided" that she was not going to marry again. She thought, "I'm old enough now to be a widow, and this is the life I'm going to have to get used to." But it turned out that wasn't the end of it. Life had more in store for her. "The problem," she said, "is when you are content with your life and out and about and doing things, you do attract other people."

This led her to her third marriage, when she was in her early 70s. "Somebody said to me, 'Are you a masochist? Do you know what's going to happen to you again?'" She responded, "Yes, I'm very aware of that, but I'm not going to cut off the possibility of good love in my life because of the fear of death."

As we grow older, our opportunities for relationship may diminish. At the very least, they change. We are no longer involved in the world of work; we don't meet people through our children; we may pull back from volunteering and committee work; we may not be able to attend events or participate in activities as we once did. But other opportunities present themselves. Offering service provides one such opportunity. One-on-one service helps many seniors stay involved with others as it also gives them opportunities to make a difference in people's lives.

Service does not have to be complicated or demanding. It can be quite simple: someone reaching out and offering assistance, making another person's day a little easier, a little less lonely. Catharine K, who lives with her husband in a neighborhood of big houses, tells of how her neighbor calls, sometimes, asking for a favor, and Catharine is happy to oblige. At other times, she just stops by to check on how this neighbor is doing. It's a simple service, but it helps, and it also sustains their relationship.

Lowell S volunteers with Meals on Wheels. In his experience, while the meals he provides are undoubtedly helpful and appreciated, what really matters are the conversations he has with those to whom he delivers them. He regularly serves the same clients, which makes it possible to get to know them and for them to get to know him. He shared one example:

I had a client who I really liked. I've spent hours talking with her. She has two "autoimmune disorders," that's her description of it. She goes to the hospital in Baltimore for some kind of procedure. I don't know what it is, but without it she dies. She says it's that simple. Well, this woman would talk and talk and talk. She had worked for the Department of Labor and had traveled all over the country. She was really into politics and knowledgeable but just couldn't move around— was wasted physically. But I told my wife, if you could bottle what she used to approach life, you could be a millionaire selling it!

Sometimes an interaction becomes service without either participant having gone into the conversation with that intent. Mildred R told of having lunch with a friend who had recently experienced several losses. Two of this woman's friends had recently died. Then she found out that a third was terminally ill and would be going into hospice. She would have liked to visit, but her friend lived in a city that is several hours away; she's not able to take such a trip. "We talked about that at length," Mildred remembered. "And I felt I was being creative in talking with her. When she got up to leave, she said, 'You're a good listener.' And she's a psychologist." Mildred felt validated as the conversation brought their own friendship to a deeper level.

Simple gestures also matter in sustaining relationship. While these might not be thought of as service, they have the same effect. One woman spoke of how important her friends were to her when her husband was in treatment for cancer. These friends checked in with her, visited, and stayed in touch during that difficult period, which helped get her through. "People

did things for me," she said. "Some people I didn't even know
that well, but they just wanted to help. That was nice." A man
spoke with great warmth about people who reached out to him
when his wife was dying. There were cards, emails, expressions
of concern: "Friends, even strangers, were of so much help; it
just bowled me over. Knowing these people cared gave us both
a lot of strength."

Several people offered music as a form of service. Music is
a language that reaches deep into realms of feeling and memory and brings responses when other forms of communication
might not. I spoke with seniors who visit those in nursing
homes or in assisted living facilities, and they bring music with
them. One woman plays guitar or accordion. Several others
bring recorded music. A woman who serves as a hospice volunteer spoke of the calming effect music had on a man who was
agitated and otherwise unreachable:

> There was a man who was wheeling himself up and
> down the hall—I was assigned to him as a hospice
> visitor—he was wheeling himself up and down the
> halls just very restless and swearing in a loud voice all
> the while—up and down the halls, just swearing. I said,
> "Henry, would you like to hear some music?" I put the
> headset on him, and he stopped swearing. And pretty
> soon he started singing along a little bit. I don't think
> words but just vocalizing a little bit along with the
> music. When I left him after half an hour, he was still
> not swearing; he was calm.

Marie G remembered that as a young woman, she was part
of a chorus that offered service concerts to patients in veterans'

hospitals and mental institutions. "We would sing with a slide projector showing the words—in those days, everybody knew the old songs." One evening, a nurse at the mental hospital where they were presenting a program asked if they would be willing to sing in one of the locked wards. "In those days—in the 40s and 50s—they didn't have medications that are available today." The group agreed, so the staff set up a room for the program and said to the choir members,

> If we say, "Leave," you just get up and follow the nurse who is next to you.
>
> We went in and sat down next to the patients and talked to them and some of us did solos—and the young man next to me was just full of conversation. When we sang, he sang along and he knew all the words. We had a very nice conversation.
>
> Afterward, when we got out in the hall, the nurse took me aside, and she said, "That soldier you were talking to has been here three years, and he has never said a word to anyone. Never." All I could think of was what music can do.

Mary R, who is 80, offers service by playing piano at a nursing home each week. She plays pieces that she remembers from her parents' generation, which is music familiar to most residents at that nursing home. Mary grew up in a musical family. At family gatherings, everyone would gather around the piano, and they would sing together. She credits that early experience with instilling in her a love of music that continues to this day and that has left her with a gift she can share. When she begins playing at the nursing home, Mary offers two songs that her mother particularly loved. So the music she plays provides a way of relating both to the residents at the nursing home and also to her family and the memories of her youth.

A woman who maintains a regular schedule of visits each week with those in assisted living spoke of how she began that practice. She had been visiting a former colleague and asked the volunteer coordinator if there were other residents who might benefit from someone visiting them. The answer, of course, was yes. "I'm so glad you asked," the coordinator replied.

This woman lives in a continuing care community where, at age 78, she is younger than many of the people living at that facility by ten to twenty years. "It's been hard for me," she says. "I'm living with 'my parents.' I'm living with the people I fled from in rebellion in the 1960s!" She is also subject to chronic fatigue syndrome and depression. Her visiting, she said, has helped her reach beyond her own isolation and become part of a larger community. The relationships she has built have helped her feel more secure and content, confident that she is making a positive contribution to other people's lives.

Because of the positive effects for her and because of the need she sees for more people to visit those in assisted living, she has tried to set up an organization of volunteers who would do what she has been doing. But the response, so far, has been disappointing. People are "too busy." Or they don't have room in their lives for anybody else. Or they are reluctant to take the risk of entering into new relationships. It's frustrating: such a simple opportunity for helping another person and for being helped. But so often the call goes unanswered.

1.

Elderly people often say they are lonely. Do you ever feel lonely?
Do you think the seniors with whom you interact are lonely?

2.

What have you found helpful in establishing new relationships?
Do you have long-term friendships that still are meaningful for
you? How do new and long-standing friendships differ?

3.

Do you seek out new friendships at this stage of life? Is friendship different now than it was in earlier years?

4.

Are there opportunities for service available to you? Do you
have experiences of service that you might speak of?

EIGHT

Legacy

You try to tie up all those loose ends at the end of life.
—Jim A, age 73

During our final years, we review our lives. What I have done? What am I proud of? What do I regret? What has my life meant? How has it mattered? What lessons are contained in this life I have lived? And what might I pass on to the next generations? We find meaning by considering both our own lives and how we might contribute to the quality of life for those who follow.

At age 77, Steve C finds himself evaluating his life and how it has unfolded. "As I look back," he said, "it all makes sense. But at the time, it was like, 'Oh my God! What am I going to do next?'" The opportunity to review is satisfying for him as it offers a chance to place the bits and pieces of his experience in context with each other.

This life review often occurs naturally in our later years; we feel drawn to remember and evaluate what has occurred in the days that have been given to us. In Steve's case, that process has been accelerated by his confrontation with mortality. He was diagnosed with an aggressive form of cancer and, as a result, was receiving treatment when he spoke with me. "It's an interesting period when you think, 'Well, these could be your last days, so appreciate them as well as you can.' And I've been doing that."

Steve referred to this as "an interesting period," and not just because of the threat to his life that cancer has posed. He is also deeply involved in activities that link him with earlier times in his life. He participates in two organizations that are involved with Nigeria, a connection that maintains a relationship begun during his days as a Peace Corps volunteer. And he is in the final stages of writing a book on food policy—how we produce and consume food. It's a book that, he feels, "is really a sort of capping on my serendipitous career. I can look back on all these things and say, 'Well, it's a good thing this happened, and it's a good thing that happened,' even though at the time I didn't think so."

He reflected on the surprising turns his life has taken. The son of a minister, Steve decided early that he would not follow his father into the ministry but, rather, strike out on his own. He discovered that he liked to write, was a journalist in high school and college and then worked for a few small newspapers in New England. But he was restless, which led to his joining the Peace Corps, and that opened new doors for him. It was, he said, the "defining experience of my life."

Yet throughout the first of his two years in the Peace Corps, he kept thinking, "Oh my God. What has brought me here to this developing country?" Then, during the second year, that thought was replaced by "What am I going to do when I go back?" Steve answered that question by entering a master's degree program in journalism. But after graduation, an opportunity appeared that took him in a new direction. He met a man who had been a reporter for the *New York Times* but quit that job to work for the government's poverty program. Steve decided that he would follow this route as well.

His friends asked, "Why would you do that? Don't you want to work for a newspaper?" But his work with the poverty program "was one of the most exciting jobs I had: traveling to the Midwest and the South to investigate and evaluate poverty programs." Then, Steve said, he "drifted" from poverty into the realm of hunger and malnutrition, working for a public interest group concerned with hunger issues. And that involvement led him to his current project of writing a book on food policy. Today, he said, the various pieces of his life fit together into a story that seems consistent, maybe even inevitable—even though at the time it felt "anything but."

At this stage in his life, Steve reports living with a sense of "gratitude and appreciation." The chemotherapy seems to be going well, and he hasn't had serious side effects. "But on the other hand," he reflects, "if I'm nearing the end of my life, I'm pretty satisfied with what I've done."

Life is ambiguous and can be messy. Looking back, most of us find a mix of good and bad: that which was hurtful but also occasions of healing, causes and effects we now understand and those that will never make sense, achievements we are proud of and things that didn't turn out so well. Nobody's life proceeds exactly as they would wish. Yet what seems to matter is not that everything we do is successful but that there are patterns of meaning linking the events of our lives. Put another way, we look for the story that our life has told—the stories that our life continues to tell.

Several people I spoke with have written accounts drawn from their life experience. A few produced book-length narratives. Mildred R identified a cluster of reasons why she wrote her autobiography, which she subtitled *An Autobiography Complete with Misdeeds*. When she went to work on it, she was feeling isolated, living in an area far from her longtime friends. "I had my cat, who was my best companion. She was lovely. And in looking back, I think I was feeling like I needed to prove that my life had meant something." She wondered, "Can I make something of my life?"

Another factor drove her writing: the memory of her mother and their relationship. It seemed unfinished, many years after her mother's death. "My mother rarely talked about herself. She would give me data about herself if I asked, and I guess she volunteered some things." But questions were left unanswered, and some feelings remained tentative and strained. "I wish I had talked to her more and asked her more questions about her life."

She remembered that as a college student, she still had the "adolescent feeling that I didn't really like my mother." That feeling hung on until her mother died several years later. Her mother had had high hopes for her daughter and what she could achieve in life. Mildred remembered an occasion when her mother approached her, and it was clear that she wanted the two of them to talk. "She showed me a newspaper article about a person who was a public health nurse, who had done some great service. My mother said, 'I hope you'll do something like this.' I think she had incredible expectations of me."

To Mildred, her mother's ambitions for her felt like pressure —too much pressure. And so "I said very little and tried to ignore it." Looking back from more than half a century later, "I resented the push, but somehow I knew she was right." Mildred reflected about the conflict this set up in her. "That was why I resisted being close to her—because I didn't want to have to live up to the expectations." But also, "I *did* want to live up to that."

And so, even though it was unusual for a girl in her era, Mildred decided to aim for medical school. It was a decision that came late in her college career. During her fourth year, she switched her major to pre-med, even though it took a herculean effort to catch up with the science courses necessary for medical school admission. But she did it. She was accepted into a program—one of four women in her class—and she devoted herself to a career as a psychiatrist, helping people deal with their worlds and feel better about themselves. After retirement, she has pursued a particular interest in the science of consciousness. "I guess I should admit that my mother was right!"

Mildred spoke of her desire to "prove" that her life had meant something. But in this process of reviewing our lives, there is also a factor of discovery: we set out to find the meanings that have motivated us and guided us into the future. And so to write an autobiography or to use some other method of bringing together the elements of our lives is to embark upon a venture that is about more than making a case for oneself and more than nostalgia. It is a creative endeavor through which we shape the raw materials of our experience into patterns that have meaning for us and that may also speak to others.

Joyce N is engaged in a project that also gathers memories and themes of her life, but her approach employs a different medium. She arranges family photographs into albums, one album for each year. She started with boxes of photos that had accumulated, then sorted them into years. She said, "Looking through the photographs taken when there was a significant event—I find that to be very enriching." Photos offer glimpses of the times of our lives. They elicit feelings and memories of what was happening then, even things that are not visible. If we mount the photos together, they come together to form a story.

Joyce reviews her life and concludes, "I think it's important to be honest with yourself about what you have accomplished. When I look back, I didn't do great things that will look fantastic in an obituary, but I did make a difference in a few people's lives. That's really all that matters to me."

Sometimes there is remorse when we review our lives. We might regret specific choices we have made or how we have handled certain situations. We might also regret our priorities in earlier years. Pat K, who is 73, spoke of reevaluating what was important to her when she was younger: "I think of much in life I have missed, spending time on what seemed to me essential at the time: dealing with worldly issues." Looking back, she realizes, "There was a lot of envy in my life. My friends bought new houses, and my friends had this, and my friends had that. It was like keeping up with the Joneses, and that seemed to me to be very important. My focus was all on getting materialistic things and making sure I had a wide circle of friends."

Pat and her husband moved into a retirement community when they were in their 60s, which put them among the younger residents. Finding herself among people who were farther along in aging contributed to Pat's rethinking how she was spending her life. Today, she finds herself drawn in different directions and into realms that are more satisfying. She said, "Now I realize my faith is growing along with my aging and has begun to bloom. I spend more time with God not because

I have the time but because my friendship with Him has more
meaning."

Now she finds meaning in small actions: "It's little things
you do that you realize are more Christ-like. Little things like
being able to listen to somebody when they need listening, giving somebody a hug when they look like they need it. Just
those little things that mean a lot to somebody else; the rewards
are so much greater just from knowing that you were there
when somebody needed you."

I attended a reception for two members of the pastoral ministries staff who were retiring from the retirement community
where I am a chaplain. Linda served the Roman Catholic residents, and she was much loved. A long line formed of people
who wanted to say a personal thank you and goodbye. Most
of them also wanted to exchange a few words, and so the line
moved slowly. Then I noticed that the forward movement had
slowed to a stop. I looked to the front and spotted the cause:
a woman had brought a photo album to show Linda and was
going through the pages one by one.

This was inappropriate, with so many others waiting behind,
particularly since these were people who had difficulty standing
for long periods of time. Some used walkers; some had to hold
onto a chair or a table to steady themselves. Others gave up and
sat down, hoping to rejoin the line when it moved again.

There was grumbling, of course, and I too felt impatient.
But I noticed the expression on this woman's face as she made
her way through the photos. I saw how important this was to
her. She needed a witness to her life, and Linda was the person
she had chosen, and this was probably her last chance. I also
recognized this as a need shared by many in their senior years:

to have others be aware of who we have been and what we have lived for. We need people to help validate our lives and make them real. We need witnesses, those who know we have been here.

Elaine S remembered that when she was a girl, she loved listening quietly as her mother played bridge with her friends. "They played at night, and I would sit and listen to the older people talk. I thought they had wonderful stories." But today, Elaine said, "No one knows my story, and I want to share it."

We held a party to celebrate the Christmas/Hanukkah season at the retirement community. About twenty-five people gathered in a small room for snacks and conversation. I welcomed the attendees and then suggested an activity to introduce us to each other: "This is a season of gifts, no matter what tradition you observe. I'd like to ask each of you to tell us about a gift that you remember—a gift given or a gift received." I have learned on such occasions that voice amplification is essential, so we passed a microphone around the circle of attendees that had formed. Each had the opportunity to share a story that all could hear.

A woman remembered a gift given during the Christmas season. When she was in high school, she and a group of friends decided to go to their teachers' homes one evening and sing carols. She still remembers the smiles on their teachers' faces as they came out to listen to their students serenading them.

A man remembered the gift of his first chemistry set, which he began playing with right away. He set his mind on producing hydrogen that, predictably, blew up. His mother was calm about it and let him keep playing. The man grew up to be an astrophysicist with NASA.

"You probably can't imagine me square dancing," said a man who now relies on a walker—or sometimes a motorized scooter—to get around. But he remembered a Saturday during the Christmas season many years before when he and a friend decided to go to a square dance. And it was there that he met the woman who was to become his wife, the companion of his life.

A woman talked about her search for a gift the previous Christmas for her son. Now in his 40s, he had worn a denim jacket for years until it finally became untenable as an article of clothing. "He loved that jacket," his mother recalled. "We never saw him without it." She decided to give him a replacement. But even in this day of Internet sales, it was hard to find a denim jacket of the type she was looking for, even though in previous years they had been ubiquitous. She went from store to store, just about giving up, until she found exactly what she had been looking for. At Macy's! On sale, too! Her son's joy at receiving the jacket could not have been brighter than his mother's smile of satisfaction in remembering the successful end to her pursuit.

One woman spoke of her annual gift to her three grandchildren. She accompanies them all to a live performance. Over the years, they have seen many musicals together, memories they will carry with them throughout their lives. Another woman spoke of a practice she has adopted for presents to her grandchildren. She allots each of them a particular amount of money to spend on a gift or gifts of their choice. Then she goes with them as they pick their gifts. Throughout the years, the children have learned how to work with this, figuring the costs of what they want, where they can get the best deal on what they have chosen, making their gift money go the farthest.

And I told the story of my family's first television set. This was during the 1950s when it was a big deal to get your first one—and our family had lagged behind the others in our neighborhood. On Christmas Eve, my father came up with a pretext to get my sister and me out of the house for the afternoon. When we returned, what to our wondering eyes did appear but our first television set! I remember the brand, Hoffman. It had a green-tinted screen. We had our pictures taken in front of the TV. It was that important.

Sometimes the stories that replay in our memories are painful. They were painful when they occurred, and while time might diminish their impact, these feelings don't ever go away. Rita D told of being one of the few Jews in her school, located on the west side of Cleveland. She remembered,

> My first encounter with prejudice was in elementary school. I came to school one day, and I opened my desk, and in it was a letter from all the students in the class: "We don't like you. We don't want to talk to you. Don't bother us." I had no idea what it was about. I went home for lunch, and I cried, and I said, "I'll never go back to that school!" So my mother called the principal. My mother made me go back to school the next day and the principal came and told the children, "We're all equal. We should not show prejudice." Then the following day, another note was in my desk and this one said, "We're sorry. Ignore the first note." But only half of the class signed it, not all of the students.

We need to tell even the painful stories, and we need witnesses to them too. The telling helps us get control of them, choose their meanings. And sharing our stories with others brings us out of isolation, makes our stories part of the community's story. We tell these stories no matter what our age, but during our final years, the telling assumes particular importance. For in the telling, we determine what has mattered to us: the meanings of our lives. As the writer Joan Didion observed, "We tell ourselves stories in order to live."

Marie G writes down memories that occur to her. She said, "I've been writing for a couple of years, writing about different things. I remember my ninth-grade English teacher took us on a field trip to Columbia University, where we got to see this machine—this wonderful machine. You talked into this gadget, and then they pushed a button, and it played your voice back! In 1944, that was really something." Marie remembers that on that same field trip, the class stopped at the Cloisters, which houses the Metropolitan Museum of Art's collection of medieval art, design, and architecture. "That lit a fire in me to *see* some of these things, to *go* somewhere and *see* them—somehow, someday. And it happened!"

I asked how she chooses what memories to record. She replied, "Just something I've been thinking about." But many of her memories involve her mother and her mother's complicated legacy to her. At age 88, Marie is still working that out. "When you look back, you get some space between you and the things that happened. You can look at them more dispassionately. My mother is one of those things."

Marie's mother could be an extremely difficult person to deal with. "One of my great-nephews doesn't even want to hear her name spoken. She was so critical of that child whenever they came to visit. There wasn't anything you could say to her that would make her stop doing it."

And yet, Marie reflected, "As I've gotten older and looked back on the life she led and how hard she worked—what a difficult life it was—she really did a very good job of raising my brother and me in very difficult circumstances. She was really quite a woman."

Marie's father was French—a musician and a used car salesman. He had come to America before World War I and then in the war served in the American forces in the ambulance corps, where he contracted pneumonia and the flu. "Every time flu season came around my father would be deathly ill, through all his life. So he wasn't a very strong person." To make ends meet, her mother took in boarders. "We had twelve people living in the house, and my father had an orchestra, played at nightclubs at night. So there was all this going on. I often think that that part of my life was lived in a George S. Kaufman play!"

Marie remembered coming home from high school, excited to tell her mother that she had learned in class that day that during the Depression their community had twenty-six families on relief. You would think, she said, that those twenty-six families could have found some way to support themselves so that others wouldn't have to. "My mother just looked at me and she said, 'Be very thankful for that program because we were one of the twenty-six families.' And boy, that took the air out of my balloon because she hadn't let on to us anything about that."

Looking back, Marie tries to sort out the contradiction that her mother was. On one hand, she could be mean and unthinking in how she treated others. "Many, many times. Too many times to forget." And yet, "On the other hand, there was no one who was more willing to help someone." She continued,

During the war, somebody would be a friend of a friend who would be in town and wouldn't have a place to stay. Mother would put them up on the couch. My aunt needed help. Mother was the one who stepped in and helped. My other aunt and her daughter needed a place to stay. They came to live with us. Mother did things for people all over town. She used to pick up the groceries for an elderly lady who lived across the street. Then she would make me deliver them, and she'd say, "I don't want to see you back here in less than ten minutes." Because she felt that the neighbor needed someone to talk to, and she needed someone young rather than an old person.

And there was a very elderly woman in her 90s who lived down at the corner—Mrs. Denman. The Denmans were founders of the town; their family went back to colonial times, and they lived in this enormous mansion. They took our dog in one time when the dog got out, and my mother said, "Go and thank Mrs. Denman and Mary [her maid] for taking the dog in."

So I went down to thank them. Mary came to the door and she said, "Come in and talk with Mrs. Denman." I went in and thanked Mrs. Denman, and she said, "Oh, I know who you are. I hear you practicing your music," and she started to tell me about how she had taken piano lessons at the conservatory. And she said, "I'll show you," and she sat down at her piano and played. Her fingers were all gnarled up. You couldn't believe that she could play the piano.

When I left, Mary said, "She hasn't touched that piano in years," and she played beautifully!

Marie concluded that her mother sent her out on these errands with the intent of educating her about other people, the hardships they faced, and how to be of help: "Being willing to go talk with people and listen. That was a lot of my mother's doing." And so—looking back—Marie has developed an appreciation of the complicated legacy her mother left behind. Her example showed Marie who she did not want to be: mean, unthinking, hurtful. Yet her mother also offered her experiences that developed her own sensitivity to others and the conditions in which they lived. That increased sensitivity has extended to Marie's view of her mother, seen from the perspective of years, and having found out more about her and Marie's own developing wisdom. She said, "I've learned to understand her a lot better than I did even just a few years ago, thinking back on what she went through."

"I don't like getting old," Kate L concluded. "Except for, you know, there really is a little wisdom that comes."

During our time of residence on this planet, we accumulate knowledge and experience. We do learn. And sometimes what we learn produces greater understanding, appreciation, compassion—wisdom. I asked those I interviewed to speak about the wisdom they have developed during their years of living. What have the experiences of their lives and the knowledge they have developed taught them that they might not have known in earlier years?

Several people identified an ability to sort out what's important from what isn't. Barbara L said,

> When I was younger I would have described myself as
> a bit of a pistol. I got very incensed over things, small

things. Little things would just really bother me, and I'd want to make them right or I'd be frustrated.

When you get older, it just doesn't matter. There's so much that doesn't matter. A question I've started asking myself is "In a year, is this going to matter?" And if the answer is no, I let it go. So now if I'm on the phone with Verizon, and I'm on hold and they say it's going to be twenty-five minutes and then it turns out to be fifty minutes—I used to be just completely a pistol about it. Now I'm thinking, "It doesn't matter." I'll do something else while I'm hold, put the phone on speaker and do something else. And the other thing is to not be so self-centered that I can't acknowledge to, say, a representative on the phone, "Boy, you must have had a busy day! I was on hold for a while. You must be really, really busy." When I was younger, I wouldn't have had the patience or the common sense to say that, to acknowledge somebody else. I would have been so focused on my own stuff.

Or in the supermarket checkout line you see somebody who's really harried on a busy day because it's right before Super Bowl and there's loads of people buying Doritos. And you can say, "Boy, this is really busy today. Wow, who would have expected quite this much?" It allows people to stop and know that they've been seen as a human being, not just an automaton scanning your items. They think, "Wait, this person sees me as a human being!"

Another person reported, "I just took a horrid course on the First World War, and I almost told the instructor, who apparently had been a professor of history, that he should *never* have taught. But I held myself back. I've learned that sometimes, nobody really needs your critiquing."

Diana W noted that she has developed a sense of perspective that she didn't have when she was younger. For her, "perspective" refers to an ability to stand back from particular experiences and take the larger view. She said, "I can see the total picture. I don't know if that makes sense, but I get more of a total perception of what's going on in my life."

Another woman observed, "I've found that as I've gotten older, I don't have to wear a brave face all the time. I can show my vulnerable side, and it's OK." She gave as an example a medical procedure that she was apprehensive about. "I said to the technician, 'I've got to tell you something: I'm really scared.' When I was younger, I wouldn't have done that. I would have pretended." Perhaps with age, we can let go of some of the expectations we put upon ourselves about who we are supposed to be, how we are supposed to appear. Instead, we can let ourselves be who we are, without pretending. One woman concluded, "You can stop worrying about being 'proper' as much as you might have in earlier years." That, in itself, can be a relief; it can be freeing. Another woman proclaimed, "I mean, I might even stop wearing make-up! I just might go without it. Here I am!"

I asked whether the perspective and the wisdom gained through years of living might be expressed as advice for those who are younger and are looking ahead to their own aging. What have you learned that might help others who are not yet as far along on this journey?

"Number one," said Susan H, "is just to say yes to life and prepare, prepare for getting old. It's very hard to visualize yourself as incapacitated. Visualize it. Think about it. What am I going to do if I can't drive my car? What am I going to do if I can't clean this house? What can I afford to do? Where will I go?"

In response to the same question, Tom B responded, "I would say, for God's sake, stay busy. Find something you like to do and *do* it. Do volunteer work. Find an interesting hobby. Read a lot. My wife does crossword puzzles constantly. Anything we can do to keep the marbles working!" Tom also identified the importance of being physically active, to the extent that one can. And finding ways to stay engaged with people. He said that he is essentially a solitary person—a composer and writer who values his time alone. But as he gets older, he finds it important to be intentional about engagement with other people. He also cautioned, "Start early. Don't wait until you have retired to develop relationships with people that will sustain you in your later years."

Dick B also advised staying active and engaged—and useful. That is, continuing to make a contribution. "You have to remain a part of the life cycle. I think that nature has designed us to be useful. If we're no longer useful, it gets rid of us." He concluded, "You have to maintain a meaningful life. Otherwise, you're just counting the days."

Prepare. Plan. Start early. The importance of looking ahead into one's own aging came up often among those I talked with. The phrases "Don't wait too long" and "I waited too long" were frequently repeated. In a society that focuses on youth and in which there are major industries built on hiding or denying that we are getting older, we are encouraged to put off aging, not get ready for it. Then when we come to that realization that "now I am old," many of us are unprepared, both practically—we haven't made arrangements for how and where we will live—and emotionally—who will we be during our final years?

There are the physical aspects of preparation: saving enough money for retirement, thinking about the kind of environment in which we want to spend our later years. Aging at home? Living with family? A retirement community? Working out the finances to support our later years. Barbara P prepares taxes for seniors as a volunteer. Her advice is based on having seen people without sufficient resources to support the life they are living: "Be realistic about your finances," she advised. "I think it's going to be very sad. We're going to have a lot of very poor old people."

But beyond the physical aspects of the senior years, there is preparation for the kind of life you want to have: what will you do, who will you be? Jack W advised, "Don't wait too long to prepare yourself for it. People retire and don't want to think about what's ahead. I think you should consider what's going to happen during the last part of your life and plan for that. Yes, go ahead and travel while you can. Play golf or tennis while you can, but realize that that won't last for most of us. Don't wait too long to realize that socializing will be difficult without a community around you."

And Susan H commented,

Better plan it way ahead. Have some plans in mind. I think removing clutter, both literally, physically, out of your house and out of your life, and also for your own well-being, some of the clutter of our thinking. Just be a little more patient, a little kinder. Don't try to over-think everything. Don't be quick to judge.

It's OK getting older. It's going to be all right. Everybody does it. I'm going to be the best old lady that I can be!

Bette H reported, "I find myself planning for the end more. Like thinking I really need to get all these short stories together. You always know you're not going to live forever, but now I *really know* it."

Our society conveys the message that it's not all right to be old. But the advice of these seniors sends a different message about aging. "Don't be afraid of it," one woman said, "Yes, you will slow down, and that's OK." And John G's response was, "Welcome! Welcome to the community. There's nothing wrong with you. Be grateful that you are alive and are able to have this experience! Look around you and see who needs help. Make somebody else's life better."

A final piece of advice came from Mildred R who urged, "Sing! Singing is really wonderful! It's good for the body, and it's good for the mind. It's good for the brain. It's good for the muscles. And it's good for the psyche." Mildred sings with several groups. She reported, "Every time we have a rehearsal—not every time, but usually—I feel invigorated. And it lasts for some time. If I had sort of a bad day, it changes the day."

A legacy is what we hand down to those who follow in the next generations. We would like to leave something behind that lasts. Perhaps we hope to have helped a few people live better lives than they otherwise would have. Or that we have made contributions—even little ones—to advance human society. If we have accumulated material wealth, we would like to pass that on to our descendants—or to causes and organizations that represent what we believe in. We would like to leave resources to those who will support what we have found to be good and true.

We also leave behind our values: a sense for how we have sought to live and what we have believed in. The decisions we make influence those who come after us, even when memories of those specific decisions have faded. And sometimes the effects of those decisions reach down through the generations. My mother's family name was Dege. It's an odd name for a German family, doesn't sound the least bit German. But I didn't think to wonder about it until recently, when I heard the story. Originally, the family name had been Degen. *Degen,* in German, means a weapon: a sword or a saber. An ancestor, whose identity has otherwise been lost, was apparently a peaceful man, opposed to violence. He experienced his name as contradicting his values and so he made a slight change. This Herr Degen dropped the "n" from the end of his name, becoming Herr Dege, thereby creating a new family name without aggressive implications.

We don't know much about the person who made this change, but he left a legacy. The ideal of a peaceful life has carried on throughout the generations, even though compromised from time to time by the circumstances in which descendants found themselves. From my perspective, the most significant consequence was that this ideal brought my grandparents to reject the option of going to war as Germany was preparing for what would become World War I. Instead, they came to America, where they created a new life in what must have seemed the wilderness: central Illinois. The family was saved and reborn thanks, in part, to the legacy left by an otherwise unknown ancestor.

Joyce T spoke of legacy in terms of participating in her family's story of commitment to learning and education as well as to social justice. "I have never seen myself as a writer," she said, "I've just got a story to tell." Her story involves her father, who owned a bookstore in Harlem that became a center of political activity during the Harlem Renaissance—a time of artistic creativity, social awakening, and political activism in the African-American community during the 1920s and 30s.

The story Joyce has to tell also involves her husband's family. His father, Frank Turner, was involved in the early years of the NAACP, worked with W. E. B. Du Bois as this civil rights organization was being established, and served as its accountant. He kept the organization going during its early years, thanks to his skillful management of its precarious finances. Joyce tells a story involving Thurgood Marshall, who later became a Supreme Court justice but then was an attorney for the NAACP. Marshall once came to Turner asking for expense money so he could travel to litigate a case for the NAACP. Turner told him, "There is no money." Marshall pointed to the safe in the office. "How much is in there?" Turner replied, "Three dollars."

Joyce concluded, "There are stories about the family that need writing."

Now, at age 95, Joyce carries on the work of her family through several means. Writing is part of her mission. And she is active in her retirement community, helping ensure that it is fully welcoming to those of different religions, races, ethnic backgrounds, sexual orientations. She has also conveyed the family legacy of activism to her own children, each of whom incorporates it in different ways, so that the values for which Joyce and her husband have worked continue to be available to the next generations.

Another aspect of the legacy we leave for those who follow is the opportunity we have to show younger people how to age.

It is to model for them how to be an old person who affirms life, finds what is good, appreciates beauty, continues to learn, laughs, stays engaged, looks to the future, shows courage, offers support and care and consideration to others. We have an opportunity to show how to approach death and how to die—to demonstrate that aging and death are natural parts of life and that we need not fear them.

This is not what usually occurs in our society. Mostly, we are "protected." Aging and illness and death occur in places cut off from the flow of everyday life. If we do happen to raise a question about what is occurring, the response is in hushed tones, as if this topic is not quite appropriate. We sense that we are violating a taboo, crossing a boundary. Kate L remembered her own parents and how they dealt not just with the challenges of getting older but also with the shock of the Holocaust. She said, "I'm not blaming my parents—yes, I *am* blaming my parents. They kept wanting to protect us so they never spoke of death; they never spoke of illness. They never spoke. There was so much 'not to know' for me."

The pressure "not to know" was with Kate throughout her childhood and into her adult years. There was anti-Semitism; they didn't talk about that. There was the Holocaust, with its concentration camps; they didn't talk about that. There were illness and death; they didn't talk about those. Everything was "fine." "They tried to protect us. It was always 'shh, shh, shh.'" But when we can't talk about certain subjects—when they are hidden from us—then these topics assume greater power for being taboo. We tiptoe around, careful not to bring up anything that might be improper. Kate remembers being told, "Don't talk loudly, don't act this way, don't do that," to avoid attracting attention. But as a result, "I was afraid all the time," she said. She remembered her childhood as "living a life of a kind of fear."

Looking back, we may remember moments when something slipped through that gave us information behind the "shh, shh, shh." Maybe as children we caught a hint of something that adults knew and that children were not supposed to see or hear, but we did anyway. I was a small child when my great-grandmother was dying in her home. Her daughters took turns keeping watch. I heard one of my great-aunts report to my grandmother that my great-grandmother wasn't eating, that she only wanted chips of ice. That image has stayed with me throughout my life. The chips of ice that may be all we want when approaching life's end. And I remember that there was a strong thunderstorm one night, the kind that sometimes tears across the Midwestern plains. The daughter who had been with her came by our house the next morning and told my parents that a sudden, loud clap of thunder had woken my great-grandmother and frightened her. That image too has stuck with me: the clap of thunder in the middle of the night when we are dying. But there was also tenderness when my great-aunt shared what had occurred as she sat with her mother in the dark of night, during a storm, offering comfort: being present as her mother was preparing to leave the world.

I also remember a story about my great-grandfather that told me something about life and how beauty and sadness— gain and loss—are so deeply intertwined. My father, as a boy, had won a contest in which the participants played the card game whist. The prizes were live farm animals: chickens, ducks, a turkey. (It was a different era.) My father won the turkey, which his grandparents raised in preparation for its inevitable fate. But when the time came to convert the turkey into meat, a complication arose: my great-grandfather had become attached to this bird—and the turkey also recognized my great-grandfather as a trusted companion. My great-grandfather had given the turkey a name, "Tom," and the two had become buddies. When Tom the turkey spotted my great-grandfather, it would run to him. My father remembers the turkey perched on my great-grandfather's lap.

My great-grandfather refused to slaughter the turkey. I don't know who finally accomplished the task, but when Tom was served at dinner, my great-grandfather refused to eat. He couldn't do it. As a child, I had experienced him as a distant and somewhat foreboding figure defined primarily by how old he was. But this story gives me another view, shows his humanity—the person within his very old body. As one person I talked with reminded me, "Younger people don't realize we're the same people on the inside. It's only our outside that's changing."

A gift we can give to our children and grandchildren is to show our humanity as we age. We can connect on a personal level—show that age is only one part of who we are and not our defining characteristic.

What do you want your legacy to be? How do you wish to be remembered? And how much control do any of us really have over how others will interpret our life and its meanings?

The Jewish tradition has the concept of an "ethical will" or "spiritual will." It's different from a customary will that provides for the distribution of material assets after a person has died. An ethical or spiritual will distributes the wisdom one has accumulated through years of living. Its aim is to convey values, what we have lived for, what we hope our children and our grandchildren will take into account as they make their own way through life. The practice of leaving such a will has been adapted by other traditions as well.

There is a biblical precedent for the spiritual or ethical will in the book of Genesis. In chapter 49, Jacob, who knows he is soon to die, summons his sons, offers his evaluation of each of them, and gives them his blessing. Now, it must be said that Jacob is not especially gracious in addressing his children. He is indeed quite critical of his sons and what they have become and what their prospects are. "Reuben . . . you shall not excel." "Simeon and Levi are brothers . . . a curse on their wrath because it was ruthless." "Dan—how insignificant his people, lowly as any tribe in Israel." "Benjamin is a ravening wolf." Only Jacob's favorite, Joseph, receives his full-throated endorsement: "Joseph is a fruitful tree by a spring." And yet, despite the ill-tempered nature of Jacob's evaluations, they do suggest the passing of one's thoughts and perceptions on to the next generation. Their inclusion in the Bible also testifies to the ancient origins of the practice of leaving a legacy for those who follow.

Over time, this custom has developed into a process of sharing one's wisdom, one's experience, one's essential convictions. Through a spiritual will, we may express to the next generations a sense of what we have found to be good and true, encouraging those who follow to take these lessons into account while also pursuing their own lives, finding their own truths. (It is best not to follow Jacob's example too closely: a will—spiritual or otherwise—is no place to criticize, settle scores, or try to get in the last word.)

When I plan a memorial service, I always ask family members, "What was important to this person we are remembering?

What did he live for? What would she want us to remember about her?" I often get an awkward silence in response. The survivors don't know what to say. They don't know how to articulate what was at the core of this person they might have spent most or all of their lives with. A spiritual or ethical will gives concrete expression to the truths we have realized in our lives. It gives our loved ones a glimpse of who we have sought to be, from our own perspective. Creating one gives us an opportunity to bring together the fragments of our lives into a statement of what our time of being on this earth has meant. It is a means for discovering and creating meaning.

I think about my daughter and my stepchildren. What do I want them to know about me? Everything, unfiltered? Probably not. But there are some stories that I would like to share. I want them to have a sense of what I have cared about, what has mattered to me, what I have tried to do and be. I would like to pass on something of what I have learned in the time that has been given to me and—maybe more important—*how* I have learned it. I want them to know about my struggles too, the things I have tried that haven't worked out very well, the times when I have had to change course, give up on one dream, try another. I don't want them to try to replicate my life; I also don't want them to hold me up as an ideal. Rather, I hope that something of who I have tried to be at my best will continue to live on in them, offering one source of direction and insight among the many others that they gather through their own living.

A spiritual will can be a written document. It can follow the format of a material will in which there is a message for descendants, perhaps specific messages for individual children or grandchildren. Or it can be written as an essay, a reflection of what one has found to be of worth and value in one's life. It can be a letter addressed to one's descendants; it can be a series of short remarks, distilling what one has learned throughout the years. A spiritual will can even take the form of a poem or a song through which one expresses not just wisdom and advice but also something of life's deep beauty.

I think of Marguerite R and her recognition of both the tragedy and the comedy of existence. Yes, there is much that is sad and aspects of life that are tragic, but she also shared what she has found about getting through such times: "Being able to survive and laugh with people when bad things are happening." That is, even in challenging times, we can be saved by laughter. She also leaves the legacy of love to her descendants. As she put it, "I hope that all my beloved people understand how much I love them."

Joyce N spoke of her legacy as the difference she had made in a few people's lives, rather than leaving behind great works, great wealth, great accomplishments. She said that having been a positive influence for a few individuals is "really all that matters to me." Several people I talked with described their legacies in terms of telling their stories so that the next generations would have access to them. Elaine S reported, "I asked older people in the congregation if they would be willing to talk about their life, and they were delighted to." They cherished the opportunity to share with others the meanings they have found. And participants in a class I offered on writing spiritual wills agreed on another simple value: kindness. Through years of living, they learned that kindness matters, even though it is often neglected as we go forth in our pursuit of other things.

John G and Gail T spoke of their legacy in terms of small scholarship funds they have set up. Even though an element of material wealth is necessary to support this endeavor, the real legacy, they said, is the support they offer people who are trying to make their way in the world. Gail described the application process for a fund she set up to support women. It pays half the cost, up to $1,000, for any course they want to take. Gail said, "They have to write an application stating what their dream is, how they expect to get there, where they are in the dream, and what comes next." And then they are interviewed. Gail's legacy, then, is the encouragement given to women to find a dream and create a plan for realizing it.

A legacy need not be concrete, a physical inheritance. Several people spoke of customs they had established that they hope will continue—a part of their legacy to the next generations. "Our family gets together every Friday night," one woman reported. "This has become a weekly event. My grandchildren absolutely open up—they'll talk politics, tell about courses they're taking, ask questions back and forth." Three generations gather together regularly to stay in connection with each other. That too is a legacy.

A recipe can be a legacy as well. We pass down foods from generation to generation, and when we make or eat a dish that is attributed to a grandmother or a great-grandmother, she is with us again. When our children were old enough to establish their own homes, my wife and I put together a family cookbook, and we gave each of them a copy. Our family cookbook featured recipes of dishes we often cooked when they were growing up, interspersed with family photos. I expect that, in the future, many of those recipes will look as dated as those I find in my mother's old scrapbooks—"midcentury modern" recipes that drew upon the industrial foods of that era and that she had clipped out of magazines. Yet I still return to other dishes she made, some of which have origins extending back into generations before her. When I make my mother's potato pancakes, using my grandmother's recipe, we are connected with each other across the years.

When my wife and I created our family cookbook, it was less about the specific recipes than it was an effort to recall memories of the family together, seated around the dinner table, having conversations that continued long after the food was gone. I grant that this is an old-fashioned practice in this day of over-scheduling and of ever-present electronics that compete for attention. I hope, though, that the memory of those conversations lives on for them and that they continue to value mealtimes together as they help shape future generations. I hope that the value we put on regular conversation with each other is a legacy that survives and continues to be handed down. I hope that this custom continues to be a source of meaning for them as it has been for us.

1.

Tell about an experience that helped you understand something about who you are or who you aspire to be.

2.

Do you think you have gained wisdom in your years of living? How would you express what you have learned?

3.

What advice would you offer to those who are younger, anticipating their own aging? What have you learned that you would pass on to them?

4.

A spiritual will is a statement of what one has learned and valued in life, recounted for the next generations. What would
you include in your spiritual will? Are there other legacies—
such as a tradition—you hope to hand down to the generations
that will follow?

Spirit

I just learned that the Hebrew word for
"spirit" and "wind" is the same: ruach.
So my whole life is writing about the wind.
The wind of the Bronx,
the hills of the Bronx, the moors and always
the wind.
Always the wind.
Maybe it was the spirit I was writing about
all the time.

           —Kate L, age 87

Spirit, according to the psychiatrist and theologian Gerald May in *Will and Spirit*, is "the force of being." It is the fundamental energy that pulses through us and the lives of all others, "the same energy that impels the being of all creation." Spirit, as the essential life force, relates us "to everyone and everything in the universe." At the center of existence—creating and sustaining and inspiring and calling us—is spirit.

But spirit is not directly accessible; it does not appear in response to a summons. If we try to capture it, tame it, give it a name, manage it for our own purposes, then we lose access. Even though spirit is always present, our efforts at control put it out of reach. Or the busyness of everyday life captures our attention, and we miss what may be right in front of us. Or the noise of the world drowns it out, and we cannot hear.

Something unexpected may be needed for us to become aware of the force of life. Perhaps an interruption in our lives that opens up time and space that had been filled with activities. Sometimes it's an unanticipated change when our plans are thrown into disarray, and for a time we find ourselves exposed: unguarded, unprotected, undefended. Sometimes it's reaching a dead end in executing a plan or trying to live a dream, and then we don't know what to do next. Sometimes it's disillusionment: what we had believed to be true comes up short, and then we find ourselves questioning. We become open and available.

Bertrand Russell witnessed the suffering of his friend Evelyn Wade Whitehead as she endured an attack of angina, and he was struck by the loneliness of the human condition. In his autobiography, he writes that he also became aware that this isolation can be penetrated by "the highest intensity of the sort of love that religious teachers have preached." In response to that moment of connection and the realization that resulted, Russell says, "I had become a completely different person. For a time, a sort of mystic illumination possessed me." And while its intensity diminished over time, he says that "something of what I thought I saw in that moment has remained always with me."

Deeply felt positive experiences can also open us to the presence of spirit. The birth of a child. A moment of insight. Falling in love. Deep sharing with another person that brings your relationship to a different level. An instant when the beauty of the world reveals itself, and we are stunned into silence and gratitude. Then the thoughts and activities with which we normally fill a day shrink in importance. We find ourselves present to an energy both within and outside of ourselves that brings us life, that is life itself.

People have described the phenomenon of "religious experience" (also known as "spiritual experience" or "mystical experience") throughout the ages. The everyday world slips away and is replaced by what is perceived as a deeper and truer reality. Those who try to describe what they have experienced speak of a sense of awe and mystery, of feeling very small in the context of the reality that has been revealed—and yet they also feel enhanced by the experience. They claim to have been granted access to the creative energy of life that is usually not available to human understanding and that is, as a result, difficult to express in the language of everyday life. Religious experiences are transitory, often quite brief, but they offer the possibility of profound change, challenging a person to reestablish their life on a deeper and more enduring basis.

Aging has the capacity to bring similar insight. We encounter the unexpected ("I am surprised to be so old. I didn't expect it to happen to me"). The things we took for granted throughout our lives—people and objects and activities we could do and roles that defined us—have changed or are no longer available to us. ("Aging is about loss.") We realize, on a personal level, that change is of the nature of things. ("I hate looking in the mirror. I don't see any of *me* there.") We find ourselves vulnerable, dependent; we are revealed as creatures subject to forces greater than we ourselves can control. Then the illusions we rely on to get us through our days ("I am in charge," "I can be anything I choose to be," "I am the master of my destiny") slip away.

Some are devastated by the changes aging brings and what those changes reveal about the foundations upon which they have built their lives. But others find in such changes a portal offering them access to deeper currents of existence. In Gerald May's words, they encounter the "force of being" that connects us "with each other, with the world around us, and with the mysterious Source of all." While that encounter can be terrifying, we may also respond with appreciation. And with awe.

"Gratitude has been filling my life and sometimes spilling out of my eyes," Miki R told me. Much of her time and energy are now consumed by taking care of her husband, who is ill and in a nursing home. She is coming face to face with the reality of aging and its effects on her body and her own mortality as she cares for her ailing husband. And yet it is precisely at this point in her life that she is realizing something true and even transforming. "I want to read something to you. I forget where I found it," she said. "'Sometimes our lives have to be shaken up, changed, rearranged to relocate us to the place where we're supposed to be.' That is what my life has done. It's relocated me. I wrote under that quotation, 'Why did it take so long?' Why did it take me almost eighty years to get here? Because I *really like* where I am! I'm sorry that my husband has to be diminished in the way that he is, but the process I'm going through is proving to be a gift."

Ruach, the Hebrew word for "wind" and for "spirit," is also the word for "breath." Wind and spirit and breath are expressions of the life force that flows through each of us and all of us. When we are young, we may take breath for granted. It's just what we do: we breathe. Similarly, the wind is a feature of ordinary life: sometimes pleasant, as a summer breeze; occasionally destructive, when a storm tears through. But mostly an everyday occurrence that we notice occasionally but usually don't.

It might take the perspective of age to acquaint us with the miracle of breath and the wind that brings us life and relates us to spirit—that connects us with all that is. We listen for the wind. We breathe with appreciation. And with each breath, we participate with gratitude in this life we so mysteriously share.

"Always the wind," Kate L observed. "Maybe it was the spirit I was writing about all the time."

NINE

Letting Go

*It was such a liberating feeling! I felt like I was myself
and that I had gotten my old self back for
the first time in sixty years.*
—Marie G, age 88

When he was in his 50s, my grandfather had a heart attack. It made him a better person. Also, I think, happier and more content. His heart attack probably saved his life.

My grandfather was a furniture maker who specialized in original pieces that replicated antique designs. It was exacting work, and his business was highly susceptible to changes in the economy. He sought to maintain control, but sometimes he couldn't, and then he would explode. My mother remembered, "He would get *so angry*."

Then the heart attack. His doctor advised him to let up, take life easier, let go of his demand to always be in charge. My grandfather was a good patient; he took his doctor's advice seriously. He taught himself to let life happen as it was going to happen. He learned perspective. He dealt with what was in front of him rather than getting angry when things weren't going his way. By the time I was a teenager, his business had slowed, and he did most of the skilled work himself. I spent afternoons in his shop, helping out. I remember watching him perform a delicate operation on a piece of furniture, and something would slip, crack, break—which might have previously thrown him into a rage. But now he would shrug, take a deep breath, start again.

This change in attitude changed him. For one, he lived another twenty-five years after his heart attack. For another, he became more willing to let life proceed on its own terms rather than trying to bend it to his will. As a result, he became easier to live with and, I think, more satisfied with his life. By letting go of his perfectionism and of the desire to be fully in control, he was able to live better and longer.

Gerald May noted in *Will and Spirit* that deepening one's spiritual life is often not a matter of doing more but of doing less: "not with the addition of something, but with subtraction." We let go of possessions and attitudes. We simplify. We learn to live with limitations. We pull back from the everyday busyness with which we had filled our lives. That is, we engage in a process of subtraction, letting go of distractions, clutter, compulsions, "stuff" we don't need any more—so that we may be more present to what is before us and appreciative of what is.

Artists, in creating a work, often proceed by getting rid of what distracts from the central message they want to convey. Consider a photograph used by a painter to record an initial impression of a scene. The finished painting has less detail than the photograph, but the image on the canvas makes a stronger impression. Similarly, writers and storytellers strengthen the impact of their tales by removing elements that do not contribute to the story they tell.

Throughout the generations, those who have entered a path of spiritual development have been taught to start by letting go. They let go of what keeps them stuck and anchored in their everyday lives so that they can be open to wider and deeper truths of existence. Those who meditate let go of distractions that enter consciousness as they seek to be present, here and now. Those who undertake a pilgrimage start by discarding anything that might weigh them down on the journey they are undertaking, whether it be possessions or attitudes or their personal identity. Muslims who undertake the pilgrimage to Mecca shed symbols of wealth, culture, class, and life accomplishments, putting on sandals and plain white garments to enter the holy city. They let go of who they are in worldly life in order to present themselves as simple pilgrims before Allah. Then, freed from life's trappings, they are able to open themselves to the life-giving energy of being itself, and they are refreshed. Upon returning to ordinary life, they retain a spiritual connection to the life force; they are changed.

The foundational story of Buddhism tells of the young prince Gautama, who was raised in luxury, surrounded by beauty and with servants available to satisfy whatever need or desire he expressed. But his protected life was shattered when he encountered evidence of suffering and when he discovered that everything was transitory, everything—even his own luxurious life—would change. On unauthorized ventures from the palace grounds, the young prince came upon illness and old age and death. He was flooded with compassion for those who suffer—which is all of us—and was disabused of the illusion of permanence. With that, the young prince was changed, now more in tune with the force of life that relates us to everyone and everything in the universe. He became the Buddha by letting go of the illusion of permanence and awakening to the transitory nature of our lives.

Letting go is also essential for those who would age well. As we proceed through each stage of our lives, we are called to let go of what came before. By so doing, we become present to what life may offer to us in this place and in this time: right here, right now. We make ourselves available to life's renewing energy.

"Can I talk about the *joys* of downsizing?" Charles K asked. "You can't be too tied to location or possessions or those things or you're not going to be able to change and have a good life. So if the most important thing in your life is your home and your neighborhood, you're not going to be happy then when it comes time to move."

Many of the seniors I spoke with raised the topic of downsizing, which they saw as both a necessity and a challenge as they have aged. The term refers to the process of discarding possessions and moving into smaller living quarters when reaching the stage of life when we don't need as much room, when we don't need as many things, and when we no longer want to be responsible for as much space and as many objects as we have previously been concerned with. For some people—perhaps most—it's difficult, often wrenching, to decide what to keep and what to let go of. For many, it feels like confirmation of the losses that come with age.

Downsizing can mean leaving a house that was home throughout one's adult life. It has been where the children have grown up, the site of family gatherings, a place associated with joys and sorrows, memories, and even one's identity. Our homes remind us of who we have been and who we are. And so for many people, downsizing is dreaded and delayed—not an occasion for the "joy," as Charles cited.

I have seen people move from big houses to apartments. Then from apartments to smaller apartments. Then from small apartments to one room in the assisted living section of a retirement community. Each time decisions had to be made: what to let go of, what to keep. Often what's left are a few framed photographs on the wall or filling a windowsill. And a piece of furniture or two, dating back to that first big house.

The need to make these decisions sneaks up on some people. Suddenly, it's time: an injury or an illness makes the house impractical—stairs you can no longer negotiate, a kitchen that doesn't accommodate a walker, a property in the suburbs where you have to drive to get anywhere. A location that once felt expansive and freeing now becomes isolating, and you find yourself relying on others for rides, for shopping, for getting to doctors' appointments. Or financial reality sets in, and it's too expensive to maintain the old place. Sometimes the "stuff" of one's life accumulates until what was once a welcoming home now becomes overwhelmed by piles that have built up and perhaps by a musty smell signifying that things have not been moved in a very long time. When I was a young child visiting aging relatives, I came to associate their houses with a disheveled look and a stale odor. As Barbara M observed, "I think *clutter* and *senior citizen* go together." Then when circumstances intervene to force a move, the downsizing involves sorting through the mess, which makes the project especially challenging and distressing.

Others look ahead; they plan the transition. Catharine K spoke of how she has been preparing for downsizing before actually making a move: "I'm going through all of my things and getting rid of and donating them and trying to slim down because I know what it's like to go see somebody's home who has died and stuff is all over and messy." She didn't want to leave behind a household in disarray out of consideration for her heirs, but also because "I'm really kind of a tidy person. So I'm using that little dynamic and enjoying it."

Sometimes the resistance to downsizing comes more from the adult children of seniors and even their grandchildren. The parents are ready to be done with the big house filled with possessions and memories, but the children don't want to lose the family home. They want it to be available for holidays and for gatherings on special occasions. They want to be able to visit their old room, to store their childhood stuff. So when Mom and Dad talk about moving to a smaller place, they may feel betrayed. They may assume, "This is your job—to keep *our house* in the family!" They cling to what had been, unable to fully accept that now the conditions of their lives—as well as of their parents' lives—have changed.

For Marie G, the downsizing occurred in stages after her husband of sixty years died. He had been ill for several years, and Marie took care of him throughout that time. Care of her husband and care for their house filled her days. She said,

> When he died I was relieved for him because I know how much he suffered. And I was glad he wasn't going to have to go through any more of that. He was such a wonderful, nice person that you couldn't do enough for him. To see him suffer was really hard and so in some

ways it was a relief to see that suffering end. But then there was "Okay, what do I do now?"

I was in the house with ten rooms to rattle around in by myself. And to take care of. As he had been ill for a number of years before he died, I had gradually assumed more and more of the responsibilities for myself, dealing with things that happen in the house and contractors and things. I knew better than my husband did at that point who to deal with and what to do.

Marie's two sons encouraged her to consider moving to a smaller place. They realized the toll that the house and its care were taking on their mother. And Marie too gradually came around. For the two years after her husband died, she said, "I felt as though I was on a treadmill going nowhere." Even though she anticipated that it would be painful to leave her house and the years of her life that it represented, it was time to let go.

And so she made arrangements to sell the house and move into an apartment in a retirement community. On the day of the move, she thought, "I'm going to be so sad to leave." But when she walked into the door of her new apartment— in which her furniture had already been placed—she was surprised. What she felt was relief, not sadness. "I felt as though part of the weight of the world had been lifted from my shoulders. I had never realized until that moment how much of a burden the house had become."

By letting go of the house and all it represented, she was able to be herself again. "It was such a liberating feeling! I felt that I had gotten my old self back for the first time in sixty years." She reflected, "So much of my life was tied in with other people's lives. Now I have the freedom to think, 'What do *I* want to do?' 'What makes *me* happy?' I don't have to worry whether I'm making everyone else in the family happy. That's nice."

Recently, there has been another "letting go" for Marie. She decided it was time to sell her car and surrender the freedom that comes from having a vehicle at her command. "It's a challenge," she said, "but I caught myself doing some really dumb things when I was driving. I thought, 'If I *caught* myself doing this, how many times have I done something that I didn't notice?' I could never live with myself if I caused an accident and hurt somebody when I knew that maybe I shouldn't be driving."

Marie's financial advisor, when he heard she had given up her car, gave Marie a smartphone with the Uber app already installed, telling her, "This is your ticket to freedom."

I asked, "Have you used it?"

"Twice. Once to take my old plates to the motor vehicle office, which I thought was pretty funny!"

We sort through the elements of our lives, determining which to keep and which we can let go of. There are objects we have accumulated and homes we have lived in and achievements we have attained and a reputation we have built. There are also memories: recollections of times, places, events, people. Some of these are pleasant to revisit and recall. Others are not. We remember difficult times, and we encounter regrets. No one gets through life without experiencing pain; no one gets through life without causing pain. Doing things that we later regret is a normal part of the human experience, and sometimes, as we survey our lives, those occasions return with surprising force.

Doris F commented that at this stage in her life, she remembers the regrets most intensely: the times when she failed to live up to her standards of who she sought to be. She wonders why the emotional intensity of those occasions lives on, some fifty years after the events in question. But the times she was good (she assured me that there were many more of these) have largely faded from her memory.

In looking back, we remember actions we regret. Sometimes it's not too late to rectify them—to offer an apology, try to make things right. But usually that opportunity is long gone. When I was a graduate student, I rented the downstairs of a beautiful home with the understanding that I would take care of it while the owner was moving to another city. I think I was a fairly good custodian of the property until the very end, when friends came over, and we had too much wine late into the night, and I was moving out of the house—and out of town—the following morning. Let's just say that I didn't leave the house in the condition it should have been in.

That was more than forty years ago. The woman who rented me the house was, at that time, entering retirement. She is probably long dead. But I still cringe when I think of it. I never actually heard from her. For all I know, she regarded the state of the house when I left it as customary wear on a rental property. A cleaning service could have rectified the situation. But I remember with regret. I did not hold up my end of the bargain.

Religious traditions have incorporated the experience of regret and the need to address times when we have fallen short—occasions when we have hurt someone either knowingly or unknowingly, when we have made bad decisions, when we have failed to act when action was called for, when we have not been faithful to our best selves. In the Jewish tradition, there is the annual observance of Yom Kippur, a time of repentance observed by fasting, praying, and seeking forgiveness from those one has wronged in the previous year. In the Roman Catholic tradition, confession of sins is a sacrament through which one is reconciled with God after having violated God's commandments and fallen short of what is expected of Catholics. And in Buddhism, forgiveness is a route to reconciliation both with other people and with one's own deeper self. Buddhism reminds us that failure to forgive harms not just the community but one's ability to live in harmony with the force of life.

I think about my own actions that I am not proud of: that have hurt others, that have not represented who I want to be, that have been inconsistent with values I believe in and try to promote. I feel regret, yes. But with age, I also recognize my own arrogance in assuming that I should have the intelligence, the character, and the power to glide through life without ever causing harm, without ever bumping into anybody else. That I should be able to avoid doing anything that might cause suffering. That I should never fall short of what is expected of us as human beings. The fact is, though, I don't have that power. Nobody else does either.

Elaine S said, "I have learned that you can forgive yourself. You can make mistakes." And while that may seem obvious, actually realizing it—accepting it—might take years of living to achieve. "For a while, I worked very hard at being perfect. As I've grown older, I have more and more forgiven myself. You know: I am who I am."

I would like to reach that level of acceptance of myself, but I admit that I'm not there yet. I would like to shed my self-doubt, my habit of beginning the day with an edge of dread rather than openness to what might be available to me. I would like to let go of my worry about what people think. I would like to let go of my need to live up to who I believe I should be, to prove myself, to be accepted, to shed the awkwardness with which I enter too many situations. Much of my life has been used up in worrying about things that the perspective of age reveals to not matter as much as I had thought. I've had to admit that nobody else much cares if I live up to my own expectation of who I should be—nobody is keeping score. So instead, I would like to learn how to just be.

As we age, we have the opportunity to relax into an acceptance of who we are, flaws and mistakes and instances of poor judgment included. And as we face our own mortality, we receive a powerful lesson about our limitations. A Jewish woman observed, "What I have learned from my Catholic friends is to accept the fact that I'm not in control. That's such a simple thing to say. It's so corny! Everyone says, 'I'm not in control; I have no control.' Well, you don't really believe it until there's a time when: Yeah!"

This need for acceptance is underscored by the physical limitations we encounter as we age. We can't do what we were once able to do. Maybe it's running several miles a day—but then the knees announce that they are no longer up to the task. Maybe it's trying to get by on four or five hours of sleep a night—more feasible when we are young. Maybe it's shoveling snow or taking long road trips or moving furniture or eating a heavy meal at 9:00 p.m. and expecting to sleep that night. At various points in our lives, we are confronted by limitations. What we were once able to easily do is no longer possible or, at least, not wise.

Those who age successfully learn to make adjustments that enable them to continue participating in life, even if not as actively as in their younger years. "It's OK to be where I am," Miki R observed. "That may be one of the gifts of being as old as I am. Yes, I get tired; yes, I get annoyed; yes, things can be difficult; yes, I've got scrambled eggs in my head. It's OK."

And Susan H told me, "My biggest discovery about aging and how to handle it is to be generous to yourself, emotionally. Just give yourself a break. Don't fight the fact that you're older. It's OK to be older. It's just fine."

When we recognize our limitations, when we let go of possessions and expectations, when we downsize, when we are able to accept who we are at the stage of life we are in, then something surprising may occur: we find support. We find that we are not alone, not completely on our own. People turn up to help. Our own inner resources kick in. And the force of life itself sustains us, guides us, renews us, sometimes even carries us along.

Barbara M spoke of her training to become a minister, which included serving as a hospital chaplain. Her supervisor would supply her with a list of rooms to visit. She would not have any information about the patients in these rooms, not even their names. "To not even know their name: that's really walking into it cold," she said. "But it helped me develop a sense that stepping into someone else's reality is like stepping off a cliff and knowing you won't fall. So you can't plan it out; you can't prepare. You walk into their space, and you be with them. And what happens, happens."

This experience of letting go, walking into the unknown, and then finding support provides Barbara with a pattern that she has experienced in other realms of her life as well and that, she finds, grows stronger with age. She said, "I feel the universe holding me. And times along the way when I'm not sure what to do or how to manage something—not always but many times—it just works out. Whatever help I need, it is there. Even when it doesn't appear to be. The more I trust that and the more I listen to it, the stronger that sense is becoming."

Kate L told of an encounter with a friend, outside, on a warm day:

> I knew she had cancer. And it was a sunny, beautiful day. There was a bench right out there, and I was walking through the garden. She had on a big bonnet, she had a kerchief underneath because she had lost her hair. And her face was skeletal. Her whole body was skeletal, very thin, but she had her face in the warmth of the sun. I sat down next to her, and I asked if I could talk to her.
>
> She said, "Yes, of course." I asked her how she had the courage. It was her second round [of cancer treatment]. How did she have the courage? And she gave such a simple answer. She said, "I just give it over to God."

Kate went on to say that she has great respect for how her friend dealt with cancer, even though hers is not Kate's own faith: "I have a different thing. I have a tremendous feeling about being Jewish." For her, letting go involves entering the stories and the traditions and the music of her people. She lets go of her efforts to be in control and admits herself into the flow of a larger story, a tradition, a community that has stood strong through the generations and that now offers her support and guidance, drawn from the well of more than 3,500 years of Jewish history.

I asked JoWynn J if she had any advice for those facing their own aging—advice either from her own experience or from that of the elderly people she visits in assisted living facilities. She advised being intentional about letting go. "I know that practice in letting go is important to my contentment," she said. "As we age, we have to keep letting go. I think that practicing and being able to accept that we have to let go is something people can do to accept their own aging."

Elaine S spoke of one realm in which her resistance to aging has played out: riding the bus or the subway. Earlier, if someone offered her a seat, she would decline, interpreting this courtesy as an insult—a judgment of her infirmity. "I used to fight it," she said, "before I decided, hey, it's OK. That's part of living with who you are. So now when a person gets up and says, 'Oh, won't you have this seat?' I accept." "It's very nice when some young teenager holds the door for me. I say, 'Thank you, young man. This is lovely!'"

Spiritual practices such as meditation and mindfulness begin with letting go. We let go of the distractions that usually occupy our attention as our mind darts from one topic to the next and then the next and the next. In meditation, we shed that mental restlessness as the mind relaxes, and the body follows. Then, with practice and patience, we find ourselves becoming quiet, calm, attentive. And sometimes—not always, but sometimes—there are intimations of what we sense as a deeper state of being. We encounter the flow of life itself, which runs through each of us and through all of us and through the world itself, sometimes called "the river below the river." In it we may find support, guidance, renewal that some call divine love and that others prefer not to name at all.

Gerald May called the state that we enter by letting go "a special kind of *not-knowing*" that is "based more on appreciation than on comprehension." Rather than trying to understand and control, we learn to accept, to appreciate, to be. And sometimes, the most fertile spiritual condition is simply acceptance that we don't know. We reach a point in life when our familiar scripts don't work and what has made sense until now doesn't anymore. Or we may face flaws in our outlook that have always been there but that we never realized or admitted. Even though we might, in response, choose to double down on what, for us, has always been, we can also accept and affirm our lack of understanding, which allows for a new openness. In approaching our days with the attitude of "I don't know," we may find openings into realms we have not previously experienced.

Marie G observed that since moving out of her house and entering a new community, she has found herself in new and uncharted territory, doing things she had never done before. She is surprised and pleased that now, at age 88, she finds that "life has been full of 'I really haven't done this before.'"

Another way to practice letting go is through humor. Laughter keeps us from taking ourselves too seriously. It brings perspective to our worries and anxieties; it protects us from being overwhelmed. Humor offers freedom from everyday concerns that can tie us down and challenges that can sap our spirit.

A woman in the early stages of Parkinson's disease talked about the limitations this condition is beginning to place on her—and what she has found to help. "I drop things, of course, all the time," she said. "It depends partly on the mood I'm in

at the time and how much energy or fatigue I have, but I'm
more likely to laugh about it than I am to be angry." She said
that she's always been able to laugh at herself, which has been
a resource in difficult times. "If you're able to laugh at yourself,
it's a big help. A big help."

"Oh, I like humor," Mildred H told me. "I laugh all the
time. I find life very ludicrous and I find it very funny. Other
people may be sobbing, but I'm laughing. There's nothing
wrong with me, but I prefer to see the light side rather than
the dark side." Her advice to younger people: "Just laugh a
lot. Laugh a lot." And Tom B observed, "I don't like to hang
around with people who don't have a sense of humor about
themselves and about the world and a sense of irony. I guess
a sense of humor is a common characteristic of people whose
aging we so admire."

Perhaps humor feels inappropriate when addressing serious
issues like aging and illness and death. And throughout the ages,
there have been warnings about the perils of laughter. In 1748
the English Lord Chesterfield wrote, in a letter to his son, "Having mentioned laughing, I must particularly warn you against it;
and I could heartily wish that you may often be seen to smile, but
never heard to laugh, while you live. Frequent and loud laughter
is the characteristic of folly and ill manners." And remember the
tale of the Three Little Pigs: the two of them prone to laughter
and merriment find themselves at risk of being swallowed up by
the Big Bad Wolf. They are saved by the intervention of their
sensible brother, who proclaims as his motto, "I build my house
of stones, I build my house of bricks, I have no chance to sing
and dance for work and play don't mix."

In a *Psychology Today* column, Pamela Gerloff stated that
the average 5-year-old laughs three hundred times per day, but

the average 40-year-old, only four. Apparently, something serious happens to us in the thirty-five years between 5 and 40—so serious that we cease finding much very funny anymore. As we grow older still, we might want to reevaluate that stance. For, according to John Morreall in his book *Humor Works,* humor has benefits that extend beyond the immediate pleasure of a good laugh.

It has physical benefits, writes Morreall: "Laughter gives the lungs a workout. When we laugh heartily we take in six times more oxygen than when we are talking. In fact, simply smiling makes it easier to breathe." Laughter has also been shown to be effective in controlling pain. "In one experiment medical students were told to put their arms in ice water and keep them there as long as they could. Those who did not joke about this, who could find nothing funny in this exercise, had to pull their arms out quickly. While those students who cracked jokes about whatever must be going on in this experiment were able to hold their arms in the icy water twice as long."

Humor reduces stress. On the website of his company Humor That Works (www.humorthatworks.com), Andrew Tarvin describes how Abraham Lincoln used humor to deal with the terrible pressures he lived with, but he was severely criticized for making jokes during such a serious time. Once he became fed up and unloaded his frustration onto his cabinet: "Gentlemen, why don't you laugh? With the fearful strain that is upon me night and day, if I didn't laugh I would die. And you need this medicine as much as I do."

"We do a lot of gallows humor," a resident in a retirement community reported. "We pass each other in the hall: 'How are you?' 'Oh, I'm still erect!' Or 'Better than the alternative!'" And while there is an edge to the humor, it still keeps us from becoming mired in the afflictions of our lives. When we can laugh about our struggles, we retain our own identity. We claim the power to write our own story.

Loss of memory provides occasions for quips that reveal an underlying anxiety but that also enable us to rise above the worry. "I can't say much about memory," Marie G said. "I can't remember having one that worked!"

I overheard a conversation between two women in the hall at the retirement community where I work. One said to her friend, "How are you today?" She replied, "Oh, about the same as yesterday."

The first woman persisted. "Okay. So how were you yesterday?"

The reply: "I don't remember!"

And it struck me as very funny. As we age, we often fear losing our memory. We forget a name and immediately conclude that dementia is knocking at the door. And indeed, research reported in the *New York Times* shows that this fear actually makes it more likely that we won't remember. When we become anxious about remembering, we are more likely to forget.

So this woman's response to her friend's query was just right; she made a joke about her memory loss. In so doing, she refused to feed her own anxiety about it. She rose above this fact of her existence at this stage of her life.

After I presented a program on aging, a man who said he had grown up in Africa offered an African saying. "We laugh," he said, "to keep the sky from falling."

1.

What have you had to let go of as you have aged? How has that affected you?

2.

Have you had the experience of downsizing? What were its challenges? What opportunities presented themselves as you went through the process?

3.

In remembering the experiences of earlier years, do you sometimes return to regrets? What do you do with the regrets that turn up?

4.

Can you remember a time when you made a joke or laughed about how aging was affecting you? Share it with someone.

TEN

Presence

I used to think, "I can't wait to get this done
so that I can get on to the next thing."
I don't do that anymore.
—Barbara L, age 75

"Recently, my life has entered a new stage, one that is more contemplative," Jim A said. He finds himself evaluating his priorities, how he spends his time, and considering what is really important to him. "I'm thinking about where I've been, where I'm going, what I'm doing." He has stepped back from the activities that have previously claimed his attention, and he is now exploring different realms. "I have begun to realize, more and more, the value of living 'in the moment.'"

Jim told me about his life up to this point: a career with the Navy in research and development, marrying and raising children, establishing economic security, achieving success in his fields of endeavor. When he retired from the Navy, he and his wife established a small business. At the same time, he became involved with several nonprofits: his church, the local Democratic Committee, and community organizations. After ten years, he and his wife closed their business, but Jim continued his involvement in "charitable, political, and faith-based endeavors that would assure a legacy." Looking back, he described a busy and productive life. "I was totally focused and committed in whatever I happened to be doing at the moment."

But then something changed. "All of a sudden, I began to realize: I'm 73 years old! And my wife and I are sitting here thinking we're living in a big house, just the two of us, and, well, this is silly. We both should be thinking about downsizing." He decided to curtail his involvement in several community organizations. He still believed in their missions but could no longer summon the energy he once had for those endeavors.

Besides, while he had been so busy in community work, he had also been neglecting his health. "I was overweight at 235 pounds; I was technically obese. My diabetes was getting into trouble. My numbers kept on going up, and they maxed out my drugs. So I started working out, exercising, reading up on diet, changing the way I eat, and now I run every day. Lost 25 pounds and feeling great."

These changes prompted him to begin evaluating how he had been living and how that might change. "I started thinking: All my life I've been Type A, and my entire career I've been working and working, and I've never really taken time to relax. I used to go on vacation and take briefcases full of material with me! I have come to realize that my sole attention during my earlier years on success and achievement blinded me to the benefits of what I have come to understand as 'mindfulness.'" Jim has started meditating, which has helped turn his attention toward becoming "more appreciative and attentive." He said that it's not easy and that he is "only beginning to recognize the benefits." And yet, he said, "I am happy, feeling better than I have in a long time."

Looking around at others in his age group, Jim sees "so many who are lost or misdirected or uncertain as to what their worth is. And they are trying to prove something." But now he realizes that "a lot of things that I thought in the past were important are no longer really important." At this point in his life, he said, "I've got nothing to prove to anyone."

Jim quoted the poet Maya Angelou: "We spend precious hours fearing the inevitable. It would be wise to use that time adoring our families, cherishing our friends, and living our lives."

The later stages of life offer an opportunity to refocus our attention and enter a more reflective mode of being. It seems a natural progression. After letting go of jobs and responsibilities and roles and possessions, we find ourselves becoming more present to what is, right here and right now, often finding that in the rush of our earlier years, we missed much of life's beauty and richness.

Some ascribe this change in outlook to the realization that their time remaining in this life is shrinking. May Sarton writes in *At Seventy: A Journal* that she took that milestone birthday as a "warning." For her, it was a call "to make every effort to live in eternity's light, not in time." She strove "to live in the moment, the moment unalloyed—to allow feeling to the limit of what can be felt, to hold nothing back." The awareness of her own approaching death brought a new urgency to life in the time she had left, an admonition not to waste it.

In a similar vein, Pat K said, "Sometimes I worry about what my last days of life might be, whether it's going to be a prolonged illness or whether it's going to be something that's sudden. That's why I have a philosophy of making every day count. Don't put off until tomorrow what I might be able to do today." And Bette H told me, "I think being older makes you grateful for what you have . . . because in the past you just took it for granted."

Similarly, Dick B said, "You wake up in the morning, and if it's a beautiful day, you appreciate it because you're not going to have too many more of them. I don't want to be morbid, but that's what does go through your head." That awareness has brought him a deeper appreciation for what life has brought him. Including his marriage: "I've always been in love with my wife, but I appreciate her more now. I realize what a treasure I have."

For many, aging reorients us to the present. That, in turn, may bring us to pay attention to dimensions of ourselves that we have not previously explored or developed. Gail T described herself as a strong extrovert, saying, "Therefore, sometimes my mouth is in gear before my brain is." But now she finds herself becoming more reflective and having more patience. She is better able to listen and be present to others and what they have to say. "I think I do that better now," she said, "just being quiet and listening." And Elaine S observed that as she grows older, "I'm going inward. I don't know if everyone else does that, but I've gone inward."

This transition in orientation from the future to the present comes naturally to some. One woman noted that in the quiet that has opened up in her life, she has become more reflective. "I spend more time on thinking," she said. Others make an intentional effort to develop their inner life, perhaps by engaging in a practice that helps shift their attention toward a different way of seeing and experiencing—becoming present to what is before us, here and now. Elaine began meditating because it helped ease the pain of a back condition. But that practice has also added a new dimension to her being: "It's inner, and it's given me a quietness of the soul." She has also begun a regular practice of yoga, which has bolstered her ability to be attentive and live in the present.

JoWynn J reported that she has developed a regular practice to nourish her spiritual side. She meditates every day, pursues studies that help her gain the full benefits of meditation, and participates in a group with other meditators. "I've read Thomas Merton and John Main and many others," she said. "I belong to a meditation group that meets every Wednesday morning. We listen to a tape of John Main talking, and then we sit in silence for twenty minutes, and then we have some conversation. We do that every week."

Others spoke of participating in groups that keep them in communication with others, deepen their understandings, offer support, and provide them with vehicles through which to share their journey. There are prayer groups in which participants practice a spiritual discipline that helps them become centered and more closely related to the source of life, as they conceive it. There are book discussion groups that offer opportunities for participants to read and discuss and learn—while also getting to know one another on a deeper level. There are current events groups in which items in the news provide topics for conversation. There are study groups in which participants explore a topic in depth, and there are groups in which participants share their stories. There are also groups in which participants simply meet to talk with each other. "Let's Talk" is the straightforward name given to one of them. And some people speak of how regularly gathering with friends offers an opportunity to get to know and support each other.

At the retirement community where I work, we sponsor a monthly conversation, with a topic announced in advance. Sometimes the topics are personal: "Your parents," "Your children," "Teachers that made a difference to you," "What you have learned that you would pass on to the next generations," "An object that has meaning to you," "A photograph from a different period in your life," "A difficult decision you have faced." Sometimes the topics have to do with larger currents in society: "A national or world event that affected your life," "The current political scene: what brings you hope?" "Social justice movements that have made a difference to you." And sometimes they're just for fun: "Your favorite movie," "A book that has changed you," "Comfort food," "Which historical figure would you like to invite to dinner?"

Some approach these conversations systematically. They put aside time to reflect upon the topic in anticipation of the meeting. The meetings become opportunities for insight into themselves and into the others who participate in the group. They are renewing, energizing: a source of life.

All these can be spiritual practices. They are means, intentionally pursued, through which we can enter a more reflective mode of existence, in which "being" is as important as "doing." We become more attuned to the flow of life through each living thing and throughout our days. Those who follow such a path speak of becoming more present and experiencing a sense of appreciation, gratitude—even awe and wonder.

"Every day is a surprise," Pat K said. "Waking up 'on this side of the grass' is a surprise." For it means that "we still have time, and time creates miracles each day."

One woman expressed this realization this way: "I really, really love small things, like—it's not small!—like the sky and clouds. I see pictures in clouds always. I love faces. I love a lot of things." She said, "I always had that ability, I guess, but it's more so now."

Miki R reported, "I find myself—it's really hard to articulate —filled with gratitude for so many things, like clouds in the sky. Does that sound silly?"

No, it doesn't sound silly. It's a recognition that can come to us in its fullest as we approach our final years. Miki summarized that recognition in a statement I quoted earlier: "Gratitude has been filling my life and sometimes spilling out of my eyes. I guess what that says is that life is amazingly wonderful."

I remember a member of a congregation in New York that I served when I was in my 30s. This was a man in his later years who would sometimes stand and speak at a congregational meeting. He talked about how much that community of people meant to him, how it was where he encountered the sacred in life. He would tear up, and his voice would become unsteady, and it was hard for him to complete his thoughts and finish his sentences.

Members of the congregation explained to me that he had suffered a stroke, and that's why he wasn't able to contain his emotions. I accepted this explanation for his awkward lack of self-control, which could make us squirm. We didn't want to watch him break down in front of us. I regarded him with compassion and understanding; this was just who he was at this time in his life.

But looking back, now that I am approaching the stage of life where he was then, I wonder if I was being condescending. Perhaps, whether or not his loss of control resulted from the stroke—perhaps he was speaking a deeper truth than we were able to hear: his recognition of the sacredness of that gathering in community that connected us with one another and with the source of life itself. Maybe that's what he was telling us, with the wisdom of age and with the insight that can come from a physical crisis. Maybe he was seeing more clearly than any of us.

Looking back through her own experiences, Miki offered this summary, drawing upon the perspective she has developed with age: "I have come to my own personal conclusion that there are only two things we need in our lives—and those are gratitude and compassion. They both spring from love. It's like a two-trunk tree, and love is the roots. For me, everything comes out of that."

As we grow older, we have opportunities to reorient our lives. That is, to change our focus or direction. The experience gathered through years of living may shift our perspectives, so that we interpret events differently from how we would have seen them previously. We may also react in ways that would not have come to us in earlier years.

The change in orientation my grandfather developed after his heart attack enabled him to let go of his need to always be in charge. He became better able to accept the flow of life, wherever it was taking him, rather than struggling to direct it to his own purposes. As a result, he experienced his life from a new and, I think, a better perspective. Sometimes, when his grandchildren were playing in his back yard, he would simply watch, with an expression of satisfaction and joy on his face. Or when he encountered something he found remarkable or beautiful, he would clasp his hands together, rock back on his heels just a bit, and, in a barely audible voice, express appreciation with a simple "Ahhh."

A woman spoke of how her outlook and interests have changed in her later years. She has embarked on a course of study to develop knowledge in realms that are new to her. "I've done a lot of studying in mythology and world religions," she said. "Joseph Campbell changed my life." She discovered an interest in developing and deepening her spiritual side and found the Creation Spirituality of the writer and theologian Matthew Fox particularly helpful. "I did some extended study in his work," she said, "and it really changed me internally. These have been studies that have *reoriented* me. I guess that's probably the most descriptive word."

The reorientation of our later years is, to some degree, imposed upon us. We retire, and life is different for us, with different activities filling our days. Health concerns assert themselves and may force us to alter our lifestyle. Age, itself, slows us down, deprives us of the strength and energy we once possessed. But we still retain the power to choose how we will respond to these changes. Will we be present to the new realities with which we are presented and develop the possibilities that are contained in them? Will we follow pathways that lead us toward new fields of discovery or spiritual deepening? Will we seek to find and appreciate what is beautiful and profound in life?

A chaplain in a retirement community in Colorado told me about a woman who had moved to Colorado, in part, because of her love of the mountains. She chose an apartment specifically because it had a mountain view. But then she needed to move into assisted living, and from her new room the mountains were not visible. The chaplain said to her, "Grace, I am so sorry about the mountains. I know you loved seeing them." She responded, "Oh, but the *clouds* are so interesting."

It is an important spiritual lesson. When circumstances change in our lives, we can look toward what is available to us now: "Oh, but the clouds are so interesting."

Each person has a public side and a private side. Our public side is visible. It includes features such as physical appearance, our families, our work, our accomplishments (and failures), what we say, how we sound, what we do. It's what we first notice about a person, how that person is introduced to us. Developing our public side is what claims much of our attention and energy when we are younger. Considerable time and effort go into building and sustaining those elements of ourselves that others will notice and, we hope, appreciate.

Each of us also has a private side—an inner dimension. It includes our values, our ideals, our capacity for compassion and care, the inner strength that enables us to endure even in hard times, the hope that draws us into the future. This is our core, which can be named the "soul"—that is, the essence of a person.

A difficulty with considering this private or inner dimension is that we can't see a person's soul directly. It takes time and many interactions to develop a sense of who people are at their essence. We see where they put their time, how they respond to failure and success, how they treat other people, what happens to them under stress, and who they are at their best. We catch glimpses of a person's inner being.

And yet sometimes, even early in a relationship, we feel drawn to someone. There are qualities about them that suggest the possibility of a relationship that goes deeper than what usually occurs. Perhaps we sense a deep, genuine caring. Perhaps compassion for those who struggle. Perhaps there is an attitude of openness, acceptance. You somehow know that this person is going to accept you for who you are and not issue judgments; you feel safe. And there is nearly always a sense of presence—that in the moment when you are with this person, there is nothing more important than what is happening right now between the two of you. You sense that you have this person's full attention.

When they talk about themselves, which is not all the time, such people will reveal a capacity for reflection. They don't just repeat their old stories but draw insights from what has been occurring that apply to what is going on in our lives and in the world today. They are open to learning, to being surprised— to being wrong. And they don't continue to fight old battles. Often, they make observations that stick with us because they are fresh and perceptive, offering something new to consider.

My wife occasionally comes into contact with a such a person—a woman, usually, older than she is, for whom she has warm feelings from their first time of meeting. Later, my wife might comment, "She reminds me of my Nana"—her grandmother. And she means that comparison as high praise. She is not really speaking about the person's age, although that usually is part of it. What my wife is saying, instead, is that she senses warmth: someone who can offer love in a supportive, not smothering, way. It's someone with whom she feels instantly comfortable and able to be herself.

I think of a woman in the first congregation I served, a retired social worker named Gen, an exceptionally kind person.

Gen spoke quietly and never demanded attention. Yet, when she offered her thoughts in a gathering or a meeting, the room quieted so that we all could hear. Gen was on the committee that called me to the ministry of that congregation, and I sensed early on that I could talk with her about anything, and she would not only be accepting but also offer insights that would help me see a problem or a situation in a different way, a better way than I had before. I somehow knew that I could trust her.

Others have played a similar role in my life. Another woman in my first congregation was the daughter of a minister. She had grown up in churches and so was well aware of church dynamics, for better and for worse. She offered encouragement when I hit rough spots, assurance that I could get through them and, more important, that I had something to offer this congregation. And I remember a woman in another congregation I served who was dying from cancer, propped up in a hospital bed that had been placed in her living room so that she had a view of the outdoors. On one day I visited her, the snow was falling, and she wanted to make sure that I noticed—that I saw how beautiful it was. She was reminding me that there is beauty in the world, even as we engage in the life-and-death struggles in which we find ourselves. Years later, I still think of that occasion when I find myself getting pulled down and discouraged by the sadness and the suffering and the pain and the ugliness and the plain old meanness we encounter. I remember Bonnie S and her gentle call to remember that there is also beauty. "So beautiful," she said in a barely audible voice as she gazed out on the falling snowflakes. "So beautiful."

Are those who deepen with age more likely to be women? Well, yes—at least in my experience. One factor, of course, is that more women live into the later years of life. But also, many men have difficulty negotiating the changes that come with age, more difficulty leaving work behind and the identity that comes with their public roles, more resistance to the physical changes that come with age. They (or shall I say "We men"?) find it harder to adapt to present reality and present opportunities.

There are exceptions. Les, whose power to use his arms and legs was severely diminished due to muscular dystrophy, began a second career as an artist after his diagnosis. He could not hold a brush but produced works of subtle beauty by pouring paint onto a canvas that had been mounted on a moveable rack. He manipulated the rack with his arms, and let the paint flow across the canvas. Despite the limitations imposed upon him by the disease, Les was able to draw on his superb sense of color and design, which was what really mattered. He was a living example of courage and resourcefulness in the face of adversity.

But what drew me to Les, especially, was his willingness to laugh, loudly and heartily, at the many things that struck us both as funny. I always felt lighter and freer after spending time with him.

He was a member of the congregation I served in New York. Because he was part of the congregation, I held back from letting a friendship develop between us, thinking that I should maintain a degree of separation from him as I did from all members of the congregation. When Les died, I conducted the memorial service, paying tribute to the remarkable person he was. But inside, I mourned the loss of a friendship that could have been. I regretted the barrier I put between him and me, constructed in the name of professionalism. I still regret it to this day.

Most of the older people I met years ago whose qualities drew me to them have died by now, and I approach the age they were when I knew them. But I still think of conversations with them, and I think of conversations I would still like to have. I wish I could have talked with one or more of them when my daughter was born, when I fell in love, when I lost my job, when I was in treatment for cancer, when my mother died. Sometimes I remember a face and what it felt like to be with that person, and I imagine what I would say if they were with me.

I am apparently not alone in this practice. In my interviews with seniors, several people reported having imaginary conversations with those who had been important to them in life but are now dead. One 87-year-old woman observed, "It helps to talk to my mother. I feel my mother more than I feel my husband [who has also died]." Even that imagined contact centers us, steadies us by contact with a deeper soul.

When I think about who I want to be as I grow older, these people from my past come to mind. People who were present to others, offering the gift of attention, full attention. Giving us opportunities to discover who we are at our best. Encouraging us to believe in who we are and who we still can be. This is a form of immortality that I can conceive of. If, in the future, someone thinks of me, wants to share something with me, perhaps even imagines a conversation with me, then I will remain alive. The body may perish, but the soul lives.

1.

Jim A describes reaching a time in his life when the pursuits that had formerly driven him became less important, and his attention shifted. Has that happened to you? What has it been like?

2.

People sometimes call upon practices such as meditation, study, yoga, or prayer to help them become more present and focused. Do you have a practice that helps develop your capacity to be attentive to the here and now?

3.

This chapter describes a series of conversations in a senior community, with topics announced in advance. What topic would you choose for a similar conversation with a group of people you know and trust?

4.

As you have aged, have you reoriented yourself, seeing things in a different way? What are some examples of this?

ELEVEN

Mystery

*She had the most beautiful dream one night. She was in a
big banquet hall.*

*People were sitting at tables, and there was music and
dancing. She saw a young man who had visited her nursing home with his dog—this part was true to her daily
experience.*

*In her dream, he came over and asked her to dance.
She got up, and they were waltzing, and she thought to
herself, "Could this be death?"*
—Barbara M, age 66

Our proximity to death as we age brings us to Mystery. We
wonder about death: what it is and how it will be for us.

"I am not afraid of dying," Elaine S said. When she was
young, she was not particularly concerned with spirituality.
But she took care of her husband when he was dying, and it
marked a turning point. He went into hospice care, and when

he was in the final stages of life, the nurse said to her, "Let's get him cleaned up. You help me." Elaine found that a loving and healing thing to do. Then the nurse said, "He can't talk to you, but he can hear. We're pretty sure of that. What do you want to tell him?"

She told her husband that she loved him and that it would be OK. That she would be fine, that he could let go. "I did that, and he sighed and died. I've never forgotten that."

Elaine is 81 now. "My son said to me, 'Oh, you'll live to 90!' And I said, 'That's not a goal for me. It's having a happy life and being of service.'" She continued, "I have no knowledge of what lies after death, and I don't depend on going to heaven." But that uncertainty does not frighten her. "I'm ready. I'm not afraid, and that's how I like to live my life that's left to me."

Rita D spoke of a similar level of acceptance of the Mystery that lies ahead: "I don't know what the hereafter will be and so I'm accepting. Whatever comes will come." She expressed a level of acceptance of the unknown that seems more characteristic of those who have lived for a long time than of those who are younger. "I'm not afraid of death," she said. "I tell my children, but, of course, they don't want to hear about it."

Sam F, who is 91, said, "I do not fear death at all." He believes in an afterlife even though he can't define it exactly. "My feeling is quite strong that we shed this physical body, and we go to a spiritual kind of aspect. I believe that there are certain aspects that proceed beyond this body. So I look forward to when death comes."

His sister died recently, and Sam said that he's happy for her, "that she's now shed her ailing body." Before she died, she told him of an experience she had involving the death of her husband. This story bolstered Sam's own attitude toward death.

Sam said, "When her husband died, she told me that soon after his death, she was lying in bed, and she saw this image of her husband as clear as day. And he told her, 'Don't worry. I am very happy, and you should not worry about me at all.'"

Jack W, who is 88, spoke from the perspective of a scientist. "I think science has it right," he said. His idea of immortality consists less of personal survival than of what he has observed about the human capacity to accumulate knowledge, address challenges of the human condition, and build a view of the universe over time, generation after generation. So even though individual human beings do not survive, we contribute to building networks of understanding that do last and that continue to contribute to the development of life and culture on our planet. What gives him reassurance in the face of death is "life and its growing ability to build something unique."

I am struck by the acceptance of death and the Mystery it represents that I have witnessed in my conversations with those approaching the end of their lives. Several people did speak of their worry about *how* they would die. They were concerned about losing their memory and therefore a sense of themselves. They worried about the discomfort and loss of dignity they might experience as death approached. But fear of death, itself, was not a strong theme. If anything, it was the opposite. Several people said to me quite distinctly, "I am not afraid of death."

A few people I talked with had a concept of what will happen to them when they die. Some expected that consciousness would continue in some form after death. Others believed that their personal identity would end. Most, however, seemed to place themselves somewhere between these two positions. They didn't have a strong belief in personal survival after death, but they also wondered if there might be something more beyond death's apparent finality.

Most appeared willing to accept this uncertainty, to live with Mystery in their final years. When we are younger, we may feel more threatened by ambiguity. We want things settled and explained. It may be a gift of age to let go of that demand and coexist more comfortably with aspects of life that we cannot fully know and that we cannot control. Several people I talked with noted that at this stage in life, there remains so much that they still don't know, haven't figured out, and don't understand. They are surprised that life continues to surprise them. One remarked, "And I thought I had seen it all!"

A benefit of the openness that may develop as we age is that we become available to life's unknowns. Once we stop expecting to understand and explain everything and as we become more comfortable with ambiguity, then we may find ourselves open to Mystery.

In this context I capitalize *Mystery* because I mean something different from the conventional use of the term. A mystery is solvable. We may be stumped for a while, but there is an answer out there somewhere that is available to us. On the other hand, Mystery is not solvable. It draws us to the edges of understanding. We can't name it, define it, control it, or harness it for our own purposes. We can, nevertheless, encounter it. And when we do, the encounter feels of ultimate significance. In Mystery, we come into contact with something drawn from the core of existence, the force of being that gives us life. In so doing, we enter the realm of the spirit.

Throughout our lives, we may have experiences of Mystery that are powerful and that matter deeply. They seem to emanate from the center of being, but we can't exactly name or define what we have experienced. We enter a realm that Miki R expressed in its essence: "I find myself more open to—I really don't know what. It's awe," she said, "and something else."

I really don't know what. In the tradition of contemplative spirituality, this is the point of entry into the realm of Mystery. We encounter the force of life—life itself—and while we cannot define it or control it, we can make the decision to accept it. In our final years, that call to Mystery may become insistent. We have experienced loss, we have changed many times, we have let go of physical possessions, we have let go of the identities and roles in the world that have been ours for most of our days, we have experienced birth and encountered death. We have become more attentive to the present and perhaps even engaged in a practice to help us develop sensitivity to what is before us here and now. And then: we may come upon the dimension of Mystery.

Miki R expressed her experience of Mystery: "There are times when my brain goes away just because something is so magnificent."

While in college, I went to Austria on foreign study. One weekend, our group hired a guide to take us up a mountain in the Austrian Alps, where we were to spend a night in a cabin near the peak of that mountain and then hike down the next day. It was an October weekend; the day was cool and crisp with the sun shining through yellow leaves, making them glow against a clear blue sky.

The first of the two days passed quite pleasantly as we followed a trail that wound its way up the mountain. First, we walked through forest. Then, as we climbed higher, the trees were increasingly replaced by shrubs and then grasses that

became sparser as we continued to climb. Then the trail crossed
the brush line, above which only the smallest plants could survive, and we walked along a rocky trail until we reached our
cabin.

That evening several of us sat together near the top of the
mountain, looking out into the stars that were brighter and
more numerous at that altitude, sampling little bottles of
schnapps that they sold at that cabin—this was Austria, after
all. We talked about how small we are in the vast universe, the
kind of thing you feel and say in such circumstances.

The next morning, our guide got us up early and announced
that we would take a different route down. The trails that led
us up the previous day were gradual, none too strenuous. Our
return trip followed a trail on the other side of the mountain,
which was narrower and steeper.

We walked to the side of the mountain where this trail
began. I looked out at the expanse of sky and mountains in
front of me; I looked at the trail ahead, which seemed to go just
about straight down. And at that moment I made an interesting discovery: I am terrified of heights.

How could I have not known this before? Well, I grew up
in Illinois where there's not much in the way of heights to be
afraid of. One can occasionally find a hill—no mountains,
though. This was different. I was not in the Midwest anymore.

It was an inconvenient time to make this discovery—here,
at the top of a mountain, looking down—but what could I do?
I continued with my group, pledging to myself that I would be
silent and brave, a vow that lasted about two and a half minutes. At that point I began to inform the others that I wasn't
happy about this experience and that I did not expect to be
alive by the end of the day. My classmates tolerated and sup-

ported me, at the beginning. After a while, though, I noticed the others putting distance between themselves and me. My fear was proving to be contagious.

It didn't help that the Austrians have this delightful custom of painting crosses at points along the trail where previous hikers have fallen to their demise. Many years later at a college reunion, I met up with one of my fellow travelers on that journey. She helpfully remembered that others in the group took to calling me the "abominable toothpick," apparently meaning that I didn't possess enough substance to keep me from being blown off that mountain, which explains why I mostly crawled my way down.

Well, I survived. I did not fall off the mountain. I remember looking down from the rocks and just barely seeing the brush line. Then as we kept going, I spotted the tree line, and then finally I was walking upright, the trail winding through a forest in full fall colors, with the day's light growing dim, the sky turning a deep royal blue, and an autumn moon rising above us.

And I felt a wave of good feeling, an intense joy. I wasn't just glad to be unexpectedly alive, though that was part of it. I also thought, "Oh, this is *why* I am alive." I sensed the pulsing energy of life that seems to exist just below the surface but that we mostly don't notice. Maybe it takes an extreme experience to blast us through—for a while—so that we can experience the intense holiness of being.

"I who am the beauty of the green earth and the white moon among the stars and the mysteries of the waters," writes Starhawk, in her book *The Spiral Dance*, "I call upon your soul to arise and come unto Me. For I am the soul of nature that gives life to the universe."

Even though I was a young man when I caught that glimpse of Mystery, it has lived within me throughout the intervening years. Now, as I grow older, I find myself drawn by it, intrigued, wondering what it might mean. Was my experience simply a moment of elation, triggered by the danger that had come before? Or was it a moment in which I encountered the source of being, a force of life that was present before me, that supports my own existence, and that will continue after I am no longer here? What might that say about the nature of this life we so mysteriously share?

The encounter with Mystery has been cited throughout recorded history by people in different places, of different cultures and different religions, in different eras, and they have used different terminology to describe what they have experienced. What joins these different expressions is a sense that there is something more to existence—something more that gives us life as it also animates the world. We may encounter Mystery at any age, but we become more available to it as we grow older, shed the distractions of earlier years, face mortality —our own and that of all around us—and open ourselves to the wonder and beauty and surprise of life itself.

Kate L said, "It really helps to talk to whatever God of your choice. God could be anything. It could be spirit. It could be nature. It could be anything. Or just the word itself which makes a feeling. The word *God* has an emanation—is that a word? If it's not, it should be." At this stage in her life, Kate is comfortable talking to God without being exactly clear about what that word might mean. "I can't go into any discussion about 'God' or 'not God.' I don't even bother to do that. That's sophomoric. Let it go. That's college."

Pat K talked of how her sense of God has helped her through difficult times:

> When I was a child, I lost a grandparent who was very close to me. I remember the nun who was teaching us religious education at the time. She said that God had a garden and His garden went from early seedlings all the way up to drying flowers, and that's what made His garden so special. I always remember that when I lose people along the way, that it's this kind of replenishing of that beautiful garden of God.

Diana W, drawing upon other terminology, said, "What gets me up in the morning is just nature. I think nature is probably the closest concept I have of God. There's something in nature where I see the beauty and even the horrible things of what's out there."

As I encounter my own aging, I find myself returning with more focus to my lifetime habit of seeking quiet, becoming attentive, listening. Listening for what gives life, what I have energy for, where I might still be led. I open myself to the Mystery of life's energy, always active, creative, drawing us toward what we yet can do and be. I seek out practices that might help me draw closer to that energy.

So, lately, I've found myself thinking about the Hollywood. The Hollywood was a restaurant on the north side of Chicago. It had a big sign displaying its name in script lettering. In my memory, there were white lights flashing within the lettering, but my imagination might have added those for effect. In reality, it was probably an ordinary place, a neighborhood restaurant like countless others throughout the city (which would explain why today it appears to have vanished without a trace). But for me it became a spiritual home, a place of retreat and renewal, an environment where I would go when I needed to reconnect with life itself, the essential force of being.

I owed my discovery of the Hollywood to Norman, who served as occasional manager of the building in which I had rented an apartment. Norman also ran the antique shop on the ground floor, just below where I lived: the Scrooge and Marley Antique Shop. As far as I could tell, the Scrooge and Marley Antique Shop was almost never open. I would pass by several times a day in my comings and goings, and for weeks the store would be locked and dark. Then one night I would return to my apartment at 1:00 or 2:00 a.m., and the lights would be blazing, the front door open to the world.

From time to time, I would ask, "Norman, how's business?" "Terrible," he would reply. I thought of suggesting that observing more customary hours might help, but I kept that idea to myself since I was not sure what Norman's real business was. Indeed, he told me he was also a minister and that he gave temporary shelter to runaways and the homeless.

Whatever Norman was up to, he earned a place in my spiritual pantheon by suggesting—on the day I moved into the apartment—that I try out the Hollywood. "It's not expensive," he said, "and the cook always has something good."

John Steinbeck observed that when he was on the road, he "never had a really good dinner or a really bad breakfast." That rule held true at the Hollywood, and I gave up on dinners early. In fact, dinners at the Hollywood motivated me to learn how to cook for myself. But breakfasts were another matter. I couldn't come close to duplicating a Hollywood breakfast.

Now, I'm not talking about anything unique. Breakfast at the Hollywood was the standard American fare of eggs and hash browns, pancakes and bacon, French toast and sausage. Nothing cutting-edge on the menu, and not much that would qualify as healthy eating, either.

But health was not my concern when I had breakfast at the Hollywood. It was spirituality. Greasy food and funky surroundings can provide wonderful nourishment to the soul.

I would go to the Hollywood alone, early in the morning, preferably at the first light of dawn. I would claim an empty booth by the front window where I could watch people on the street hurrying by. I would bring a notepad in case something came to me that was worth writing down, but that rarely occurred. Mainly, I had the pad as cover to make it look as if I was doing something.

What I really did at the Hollywood was nothing. I had my breakfast and watched the surge of life go by from my window, and I absorbed sounds and smells and the presence of the people around me. I wasn't thinking deep thoughts—I wasn't thinking about much of anything—indeed, after a while my mind would go into neutral. I was just there, lulled into simple being by the breakfast and the comfort of my surroundings as the energy of life swirled around me.

My mind emptied during this ritual, yet I also felt open and present to what was all around. I may have been alone, but I wasn't isolated. I was brought back into relationship with the world and back into relationship with myself and with the force that gives us life. By the time I left the Hollywood, I felt renewed—given energy and hope to plunge back into the flow of existence.

Breakfast at the Hollywood was where I encountered Mystery during that period in my life. At the time, I was just making my way into the adult world; I was oriented toward my dreams of the possibilities to come. What might the future hold? Who is it that I can be, that perhaps I am meant to be? Where will I find meaning in my life? How do I stay in touch with life's renewing force and energy?

Today I find myself on the other end of life's continuum. Yet I have continued the practice of seeking occasions when I can be quiet, present, and open to life's Mystery, which reveals itself in the most ordinary of circumstances. I take walks on city streets, forest trails, and sidewalks. I walk through small towns, museums and galleries, historic sites, and on everyday pathways that have nothing special going for them. I walk with my wife the mile between our house and the station on the Washington, D.C., Metro where she boards a train for her day's work. Then I make the return trip on my own. The walk to the station is about communication with each other, being together, sharing the journey. The walk back home is different. It's about openness and presence. It's about listening for the flow of life and what it might bring to me on this day at this time. It's about being present to Mystery.

What comes to me now as I become present and open is less personal, less concerned with my own dreams and ambitions. Sometimes there are memories and sometimes problems and worries that crowd into my mind. But mostly this is a time of being open to life's energy, however it may be revealed. It's a time of dipping into Mystery and staying in touch with life itself. It's about sharpening my perceptions, reminding me not to take anything for granted, absorbing this strange puzzle of life in which we all find ourselves, and which we have the astounding privilege to share with each other. It's about being. Just being.

"Just a year ago," JoWynn J said, "I was dreading growing any older. Since then, that has shifted—that has changed and I'm no longer dreading it. Instead, I'm curious. I wonder how I will cope. I look at the people whom I visit, and I see how they cope or they don't cope. And I wonder how I would do. So now I'm curious—more curious than dreading."

There is a stillness that surrounds us when we are in our last days, our final hours—a stillness that reaches deeper than a simple lack of activity and is quieter than the absence of noise. This is the quiet that exists beneath the surface, and it's not completely unfamiliar. We encounter it at other times in our lives.

It may be suggested by the stillness of a cold clear winter night, when stars shine through the darkness. And by the stillness of dawn, when a soft light breaks across the horizon.

We may sense this stillness in nature: a tree standing tall in the quiet, a stem emerging from the forest floor and then a flower, stretching, blooming. Or a lake or a pond on a calm day. Even the ocean with its perpetual agitation on the surface —dip just below, and we enter a realm of quiet and calm.

It's the stillness we encounter when talking with a friend who is fully present, and the rest of the world all around us blurs. The stillness that may bring a group of separate individuals together when—for a few moments—we are all engaged, each person's attention mingled with that of the others, and the usual shifting and shuffling ceases.

We may encounter this stillness in response to a thought, a new idea, a realization that seems to make the world stand still. It is the stillness that, for a time, calms the restlessness that usually drives us to flit from one activity to the next, from one thought to another. We reach into the deeper pool of being from which we have come, that supports us and sustains us throughout our days, and there we encounter quiet.

The quiet that connects us to the stream of existence, flowing through each of us and around all of us, giving life. Taking life away. Giving life.

1.

Does the term *Mystery* have meaning for you? Does it describe anything from your own experience? What about the term *God*?

2.

What do you think happens after death? Do you have a sense of personal survival? Or not? How do your views affect your everyday life?

3.

What has surprised you as you have grown older? What did you not expect?

4.

JoWynn J said that she once dreaded growing older, but now she feels more curiosity than dread. Where are you on the range between dread and curiosity?

Conclusion

We put one foot in front of the other,
keep going, lift ourselves up, and walk together.
—Barbara M, age 66

Sometimes we discover that we have already begun a journey before actually making the decision to start. We are swept along by currents that we become aware of only by looking back. Such has been my journey into aging. I have been addressing the challenges and possibilities of aging throughout my life without fully realizing it.

At each stage, there has been a tension between holding on to what is and yielding to the realization that time passes, changing everything along the way. While I'm in the midst of it, holding on seems quite possible, even reasonable. Only in looking back do I see the futility of resisting life's energy as it makes its way through my own being, as it does through every other thing—living and inanimate—on this earth.

As a child, I watched the Mary Martin version of *Peter Pan*, in which Peter sang, "I won't grow up!" It's an anthem in defiance of the toll life takes on each of us and a pledge to resist. In the story, Peter demands allegiance from his followers to stand with him by refusing to enter the adult world and the losses it represents.

How do we know if we've succumbed to the call to adulthood? Simple, according to the song. We know we've grown up when we discover that it's "beneath my dignity" to climb a tree.

Throughout the years, that standard has stuck with me as a working definition of how I would know when I had lost the battle with aging. "Could I, would I, climb a tree? Is it now, at last, beneath my dignity?"

Even recently, those words came back when I participated in a demonstration on the Washington, D.C., National Mall. The Mall was packed with protestors, a few of whom sought relief from the surging humanity by climbing up and perching in trees. I looked up and realized that, no, I wouldn't do that. I didn't trust my ability to pull myself up into the branches and then hoist myself high enough to get a view above the crowds. Even if I could have scaled one of those trees, there would have been the issue of getting back down.

But the physical challenge was a secondary concern. It was really about dignity; it was about respecting reality. It was about honoring the stage of life I had long ago entered. Even if I could have climbed that tree, what would I, an almost-70-year-old man, be doing up there? Trying to prove that I'm ageless, immune to time's effects? I had to admit that according to the "climb a tree" standard, I'm grown up. And furthermore, looking back: when exactly was the last time I was up in a tree? Twenty years ago? Thirty years ago? Fifty years ago? Have I been grown up all this time without realizing it—without admitting it?

We resist the passage of time because time brings changes. When we won't be comfortable climbing a tree. When we don't fit in the clothes that used to look so good on us. When we aren't able to move as smoothly—think as quickly—as we have been accustomed to. When our place in the world diminishes. When younger people stop paying attention to us. When generations that follow take their turn in roles that used to be ours. When we lose family and friends and when death looms before us.

Now, as I look around, what used to seem solid reveals itself as in process, always. I have lived in my current neighborhood for almost a decade. I see high school students rushing around who were little elementary school kids when I first met them. I see people I've known for these ten years now with hair thinning, wrinkles forming, bodies relaxing. I've seen trees in the neighborhood come down, new trees in their place, now growing. House paint I applied after first moving here is now dirty, worn, and chipped. I'll have to get out and do it again. All around me I find the message of life's eternal movement: birth, growth, aging, death, renewal.

And so I return to the concerns with which I began this journey. Meaning and spirit. Where is meaning amidst the constant change in which our lives are lived? And where is spirit?

The answers I find are woven through the stories I have told in this book, even if the specifics of one or another might not resonate with your experience. Maybe you see clouds as revealing the world's beauty—or maybe you don't. Maybe talking to God has meaning for you—or maybe it's not your thing. Maybe becoming present to Mystery reveals something of life's essence to you—or maybe you find the concept too ethereal to be of practical benefit. Maybe offering service to those in need fulfills you; maybe it's participating in the life of a community; maybe it's family; maybe gardening, a book club, social justice work, writing your memoirs, mindfulness, or card games. The specifics vary.

Beyond the details of how individuals create meaning for themselves, what comes through to me most strongly is a sense of what a privilege it is—we might call it a blessing—to share in life, no matter the time granted to us. For as long as we are alive, we have the opportunity for meaning. And we experience the miracle of life's energy flowing through us.

I remember my mother-in-law, sensing that she had only weeks to live, showing the biggest smile I'd seen from her in a long time as she received a visit from her grandchildren, wanting to know what each was doing, what had been happening for them, glowing in their presence. At that time and in that place, there was meaning for her, and there was spirit.

I remember visiting a man who had laid out a set of photographs featuring his wife, who had died several years before. He introduced her to me through the photos, described how they had met, showed pictures from different periods in their lives together. Here there was meaning. And as his expression softened in speaking of her, there was spirit.

And I remember a group of seniors, most in their 80s, who had gathered to talk about social justice movements they had experienced in their lifetimes and how these had made a difference to them. There were stories of civil rights movements, the women's movement, environmental issues, efforts to guarantee human rights for the LGTBQ community, local organizations formed to help people, to protect people. In that conversation, there was both a sense of the good that had come from such involvement and of the work still to be done. The struggle to improve the quality of life in the world continued to have meaning for those who had gathered; it energized them, gave them life.

Each of us, whatever our age, has been granted a privilege almost unfathomable: to be alive on this earth right now, sharing that gift with others who have been granted the same privilege.

For this time we do have, "we put one foot in front of the other, keep going, lift ourselves up, and walk together."

Tips for Organizing and Facilitating Group Discussions

This book was created with the hope of stimulating further reflection and conversation—perhaps one on one, or in families, or among friends, or in groups assembled for the purpose of talking about the experiences of growing older. Aging can be isolating, and we may find ourselves dealing with its effects on our own. But in sharing the journey, we offer each other care and support as well as camaraderie that eases the way.

The following are suggestions for groups to serve seniors as we encounter issues that come with advancing age. The groups can be sponsored by and organized in congregations or senior centers, schools or retirement communities, or "aging in place" programs—wherever seniors gather. In any of these contexts, they aim to provide opportunities for conversation in a supportive environment. And while there is a specific focus to each of these programs as well as specific tasks and topics, they should be balanced by recognizing the equally important goal of developing relationships among the participants.

A few guidelines for establishing such groups:

- A group functions most effectively when it has a des-
  ignated leader. This can be a professional trained in
  group dynamics, or it can be a volunteer committed to
  making sure that each participant has an opportunity
  to be heard.

- The leader takes responsibility for establishing the
  meeting time and place as well as for publicizing
  the group and inviting people to attend. Make sure
  that the physical setup supports the functioning of
  the group. Usually, this will be a circle of chairs large
  enough for all to have a place, while small enough to be
  intimate. A circle with two or three empty chairs in it is
  usually a good balance. The optimal number of people
  varies with the type of group, but a range of from eight
  to fifteen is usually about right.

- In the first session of a new group, start by asking participants to introduce themselves by saying their name
  and what brought them to participate.

- The leader also clarifies the topic. Begin each session
  with an introduction to the question or issue to be considered. In some programs, general discussion begins
  after the opening statement. In others, each person is
  given an opportunity to speak before the general conversation starts. In either case, the leader may sometimes need to bring the conversation back on topic or
  to gently urge someone who is going on too long to
  yield the floor.

- Model respect for the participants by carefully listening
  to each person. During the initial round of sharing, it is

best to not offer responses other than questions to clarify what has been said. These are not forums for argument or debate but opportunities to understand and appreciate what each individual brings to the group.

- It is important to be aware that participants in a group are likely to have different reaction times. Some know immediately what they have to say on a topic. Others have to think for a while before they are ready to speak. One way to respect this difference is for the leader to invite those who have not yet spoken to do so. Another possibility is to begin each session by asking if people have had thoughts about the previous topic since the last meeting. (Some of us don't realize what we have to say on a topic until the session has ended and we are on our way home.)

- Personal disclosure from the leader gives permission for the group to delve deeper than it might otherwise. While the group should not become a forum for the leader's issues and stories, an occasional experience or insight shared by the leader can open possibilities for more meaningful conversation.

- Occasionally, an exchange may become heated, or one person will take offense at what another has said. At such times, it is the role of the leader to intervene in the interest of making sure that the group is safe for all. The leader might say, "We want to make sure that everyone is comfortable here. So let's put this matter on the shelf for the moment and consider other comments people might have." The leader should also be cognizant of anything that comes up in the session that might have upset a participant or triggered deeper feelings that need to be expressed. Often, sitting down next to such a person after a session and offering support give that individual an opportunity to talk more about what has come up.

When planning a group discussion, it is important to be aware of the accessibility needs of older people.

- The meeting place should be physically accessible to those who rely on walkers, wheelchairs, or motorized scooters. Even if a participant does not use such aids, stairs or uneven walking surfaces can present significant barriers to participation.

- Hearing loss is common among older people. Hence it is important to be aware of anything that diminishes the ability of participants to hear each other, such as other groups meeting in the same room. Any kind of ambient noise can cause problems. A room that is too large can also make it difficult to hear, as can a room with hard surfaces that produce echoes that distort or muffle sounds.

- If possible, meet in a room or facility that has sound amplification. Passing a wireless microphone from person to person helps include everyone in the conversation. And while getting a microphone to whoever wants to speak can be distracting, the benefit of enabling all to hear and participate outweighs the awkwardness.

- The time of meeting is an important consideration. Many older people do not drive at night; many do not go out at night even if they are not driving. So evening meetings, in themselves, restrict access. Often people stop participating in organizations when they no longer go out at night, and daytime opportunities are not sufficiently available. Choosing to hold sessions during the week in the morning or afternoon will serve a constituency that may be excluded from groups with evening or weekend meeting times.

- Transportation is also a consideration. People become isolated when they can no longer get out on their own. If you can provide transportation to those participants who might not otherwise be able to attend, it will offer a welcome respite to those who feel trapped in their place of residence.

- Make clear how long each session will be. An hour is usually a good length, or perhaps ninety minutes for larger groups. End each session at the agreed-on time.

I have found these groups to be joyful occasions in which we have gotten to know each other better, discovered both similarities and differences, while also putting together pieces of our experience into stories with meaning and purpose. We make sense of our own lives while learning about the lives of others. These are times of intense listening to what each person has to say, occasionally punctuated by bursts of laughter as we realize the sometimes silly, even absurd, aspects of our lives. The sharing also produces insights, and a participant may say, "I hadn't realized this before."

At their best, the conversations are not just retellings of what has occurred in our lives. They also produce insights as we engage in the ongoing process of discovering who we have been, who we are, and how we have created meaning and encountered spirit throughout our lives.

APPENDIX TWO

Using This Book with a Group

Each chapter of this book ends with a set of four questions for reflection. I hope that these questions will encourage further conversation about the issues that have been raised. One context in which such reflection can occur is in groups organized for that purpose—groups that consider the stories told in each chapter and that are guided by the discussion questions. A pattern of reading and reflection followed by conversation can produce a deeper understanding of the issues involved and suggest responses to them. Options and opportunities present themselves as we speak and listen in this shared undertaking.

In a group addressing these issues, it is best for each participant to have a copy of the book, or access to a copy, in order to read the relevant chapter before each meeting. The book is organized into three parts corresponding to the three primary topics: Aging, Meaning, and Spirit. I suggest beginning a group with a set of four sessions based on the Aging part, chapters 1–4. The first session, then, would focus on chapter 1, Loss. The subsequent three sessions would be concerned with Change, Identity, and Help.

A second series would address the second part, Meaning. Again, there would be four sessions, corresponding to chapters 5–8: Exemplars, Choice, Relationship, and Legacy. A third series would focus on Spirit. There are three chapters in this final section: Letting Go, Presence, Mystery. I suggest reserving a fourth meeting for reflecting about the experience of participating in the group and addressing the questions that came up. By this time, participants will know each other well; you will have shared important stories, important experiences. This final session can address loose ends, remaining questions, and topics on which there is yet more to be said. It also provides an occasion for thanking each other for the gifts of time and presence.

An alternative pattern—and a shorter series—would cover the whole book in four sessions. The first three would correspond with the three parts of the book: Aging, Meaning, Spirit. Then a fourth would enable participants to address unresolved issues from the first three sessions and also provide opportunities for them to talk about the implications of the discussions for their lives, here and now.

These sessions would follow a basic pattern. The first session begins with participants introducing themselves by giving their names and talking briefly about why they have chosen to be part of this group. Then the leader reads the four questions at the end of the relevant chapter, which the group will be addressing that day. If possible, write the questions in large print on newsprint or on a blackboard or whiteboard so that they are in view throughout the session and can be referred to. If you opt for the shorter series in which you cover the whole book in four sessions, choose four questions from among those suggested in each part—that is, four questions each for your sessions on Aging, Meaning, and Spirit.

Go around the circle, asking each person to share a comment, thought, or experience in response to any of these questions. After each participant has had an opportunity to speak (or pass), then the leader may offer an informal summary of what has been said, such as "Some themes I heard are . . ." or "I am struck by several things people have said . . ." or "These comments make me wonder about . . ." Then ask if anyone has further thoughts or responses to what others have said. If the conversation stalls, the leader may refer back to one or all of the questions that focus the topic for this session.

At the end of each session, the leader should note the topic of the next meeting. The leader can also offer a brief summary, closing thought, or closing reading drawn from the theme of that day.

Subsequent meetings follow the same pattern, except that instead of the participants introducing themselves at the beginning, the leader may invite thoughts or comments about the previous meeting before introducing the theme of this session.

After the initial four sessions on loss, the group can decide what comes next. One option is to go on to the second section in the book, "Meaning," with a second series of four sessions. Or participants might want to take a break, with the option of continuing later. Or the group might disband. If the group does not disband but some participants will not be continuing, the rest of the group can decide whether to invite new members or to go forward only with those who have participated thus far. There is an argument for maintaining intimacy by continuing only with those who have grown to know one another. There is also an argument for opening up the group and bringing in new experiences and insights. It depends on the dynamics and the preferences of your group.

Some time after the sessions have ended, you might consider a reunion meeting. This could be planned six months or a year later. A reunion meeting provides opportunities to catch up with each other and share thoughts and experiences that have occurred since the group disbanded. Even if the participants have seen each other regularly, a return to the format in which you have considered these concerns together will encourage deeper sharing than takes place in our everyday interactions.

APPENDIX THREE

Guided Conversations on Particular Topics

This is a series of conversations with topics announced in advance. The range of potential topics is wide and varied. Some ask for our memories. Some encourage us to think about our values—what we have tried to live for. Some challenge us to consider what we think about current or past issues in society. All of them have to do with the question of meaning: What has mattered to us throughout our lives? What matters to us now? And they involve spirit: What gives us life?

Group size is flexible. On different occasions, I have had as few as six participants and as many as thirty. A smaller group offers the opportunity for deeper sharing among the participants, a larger group presents a wider range of experiences, but both work. A challenge for the leader of a smaller group is to keep the conversation going. When there is a larger group, the leader needs to make sure all participants have opportunities to speak and possibly to keep one or a few people from dominating. A larger group might also be more prone to wandering off topic.

These conversations can bring together participants of different ages. The topics are particularly relevant to seniors who are reflecting on their life experiences, but those of younger ages can also take part. The participation of younger people brings a wider range of experiences to the conversations, which is a benefit to all. However, the leader will need to be vigilant to make sure that older participants have ample opportunities to speak and not defer to the younger people.

Potential topics include the following:

What did you learn from your parents?

What have you learned in your life that you would pass on to the next generations?

Which national or world events have shaped your life? How?

Which personal experiences have shaped your life?

Encounters with diversity

Difficult decisions you have faced

How have you experienced another person's caring? How have you expressed caring?

Favorite movies

Books that have changed your life

What historical figure(s) would you like to invite to dinner?

Holiday memories

Family traditions at holidays

Relationships with children

Hometowns

Where were you in the 1950s and 1960s?

What is a good or successful life?

An object that has meaning for you

Where did your name come from? What does it mean to you?

How did you name your children? How have you seen others name their children?

How has your generation shaped you?

Your most interesting job, paid or unpaid

A photograph from another time in your life

A teacher or teachers who made a difference

Comfort food and other sources of comfort (places, things)

In the current political scene, what gives you hope?

What social justice movement has made a difference in your life? How?

How would you end this sentence: "I never thought I'd live to see . . ."?

This list is meant to suggest possibilities, not restrict them or prescribe a set sequence. Participants in the group will be a rich source of ideas for other topics. Indeed, some of the ones listed here were suggested by people in my groups, and these often produced the liveliest conversations. You might also search the Internet for questions about family history designed to draw out stories of a person's life.

I suggest that you hold these conversations monthly with no requirement for ongoing participation, so that people can drop in and out at will. Some will attend most of the sessions; others will pick and choose. The topic of each session should be announced in advance, possibly at the previous session but also through other forms of communication: newsletters, posters, an email list, etc.

At each session, seat the participants in a circle. As the leader, start by naming the topic and offering your personal response. This sets the tone for the conversation and gives participants time to think about what they will say. Then go around the circle, giving each an opportunity to speak. If possible, pass a wireless microphone to each speaker so that all can hear. This first round is not a time for comment or building on what a person has said, but clarifying questions are appropriate.

After each person has had an opportunity to speak, then open up the conversation for comments and responses. Some people will have thought of other experiences related to the topic. Others will want to offer reflections on what they have heard. You may need to stimulate the conversation by offering further thoughts. Or, if the conversation is going well, you can just stay out of the way.

End the session at the agreed-upon closing time, possibly with a summary or a thought in response to what has been shared. If a topic for the next conversation has been chosen, announce it.

Writing Your Spiritual Will

A will provides for the distribution of our physical resources after death. A *spiritual* will is about values. It is an expression of who we have sought to be: what we have lived for, what we have valued, what we're proud of, and even our mistakes. It is intended for our descendants and aims to articulate for them what we have found to be right and true.

A spiritual will is short. It's not an article, and it's not a book. Writing a spiritual will forces us to distill the lessons of our lives into a few paragraphs about what matters most. It's not a list of accomplishments but, rather, a reflection on the meanings that we have found in living. It is a gift to pass on to the next generations. The process of writing a spiritual will also helps us understand our own lives, making patterns and meanings more evident than they might have been while they were forming.

A spiritual will can be a statement or an essay or a letter to our descendants. Some people have composed their spiritual wills as poems; some have even written songs. A spiritual will can be a written document, or it can be a video in which we speak about what has been important to us in our life. The form that feels most natural to you and most appropriate for the message you want to convey will be the best for your own spiritual will.

A spiritual will can be created alone, but participating in a group in which everyone is writing one can add depth to the final product. (It also makes it more likely that we'll actually complete it.) As we share our memories, thoughts, and ideas, new memories and thoughts come to mind, and new ideas arise. An ideal size for such a group is five to eight people, meeting weekly. This is large enough to bring together a variety of experiences and perspectives, and small enough to allow ample time for each person to participate. The conversations among group members can be enriching for all. Participants come to know one another better and sometimes learn things about themselves. After all, sometimes other people see us better than we see ourselves. Our finished will, then, reflects not just our own thoughts and experiences but the contributions of others as well.

A good length of time for each session is an hour. But as participants get to know each other, the time can go longer, particularly if you have a large group. If that happens, offer the option of continuing until each person has had an opportunity to speak, but no longer than ninety minutes for the session. When reserving facilities, assume that each session will require the space for ninety minutes.

A will is customarily opened after a person has died. You may choose this option for a spiritual will, but it can also be shared while you are living. The topics it addresses can be subjects for conversation within a family as well as in a spiritual will writing group. And just as in the writing group, all participants in the family conversations are likely to benefit from them.

Process for a group on writing your spiritual will

Announce the formation of the group through the customary channels available in your community. The concept of a spiritual will should be briefly defined so that everyone understands the objective of the group. Here is an example:

> Most of us have a will. Not many have a spiritual will. A spiritual will is similar to a regular will in that it passes assets on to the next generation. But while a will is concerned with material assets, a spiritual will offers an account of our values, what we have lived for, what has mattered to us—the wisdom we have accumulated through years of living. We are offering a class to help participants create their spiritual will. [*Time, date, place, particulars*] For further information, please contact [*name, title if appropriate, contact information*].

In anticipation of the first meeting, send the following to those who have indicated that they will participate:

> The story of our lives does not start with us. We come into the world in the midst of stories already occurring. Some of these are family stories. They can also be cultural stories, national stories, community stories, stories of our faith community, stories of intellectual or social traditions, or others. These stories orient us in the world and give us points of reference that can serve throughout our days. Think about a story that was told by your parents, your grandparents, a relative, or someone in your community that helped give you a sense of who you are.

First Session

1. Welcome the participants, and state the purpose of the group. Draw upon the initial publicity statement to define a spiritual will.

2. Invite each participant to speak briefly about what brought them to participate.

3. Read an example of a spiritual will. A good one is Clarke Dewey Wells's "Letter to My Sons," which is included in *Continually Creating Spirit: A Clarke Dewey Wells Reader.* This book is available for purchase, and the Unitarian Universalist Church of the Larger Fellowship has posted Wells's letter on the Internet at clfuu.net/quest_archive/quest/2008/06/wells.html. Search the Internet for the phrases "spiritual will" and "ethical will" to find other examples.

4. Ask each participant to share a story from their family or their culture that has helped orient them in the world and has helped them understand who they are. This is the story that the letter sent out in advance asked about.

5. After each participant has spoken, invite general conversation in response to what has been shared. Encourage participants to reflect on the values conveyed by the stories that were told.

6. When concluding the session, ask everyone to keep private what has been spoken of in the group. What someone said should not be shared with others outside of the group without that person's permission.

7. Give each participant the handout that follows. It explains how to prepare for the next session.

Note: It is possible that the group will not complete this first round of storytelling during this first session. If that occurs, you may—with the group's permission—hold the contributions of those who have not yet spoken until the following meeting. You might also plan for the possibility of an extra session or two in case conversation goes on longer than the allotted time.

Session 1 Handout
Writing Your Spiritual Will

From *Creating a Spiritual Legacy,* by Daniel Taylor

"A spiritual will is a personal statement (often quite brief) about what one has learned from one's life—created for the benefit of others. It combines wisdom and blessing."

Questions a Spiritual Will May Address:

What have I done in and with my life?

What have I learned?

What do I value?

What is most important in life, and how has my answer to that changed over time?

When have I been happiest or felt my life had the most meaning?

What have I learned the hard way that I want someone else to learn more easily?

What can I pass on to others that will make their lives better or easier or deeper?

Preparation for Second Session:

Write a story or a statement that expresses something you learned or discovered during your childhood or young adult years.

Second Session

1. Begin by inviting participants to share thoughts or questions remaining from the previous week, or that they may have thought of since then.

2. Read an example of a spiritual will that someone else has written. If possible, provide printed copies so participants can follow along as you read. Ask for responses to what was written. How does this example inform us about what a spiritual will might include?

3. Ask for general responses to the assignment for this second session. How did it go? Was it easy for people to think of an experience that expresses something they learned during their childhood or young adult years? Or not? Ask each person to share such an experience.

4. In the general discussion, reflect upon the values contained in the experiences that have been shared. Ask each participant to write down three or four values that are important to them, that have made a difference in their lives. Lead a conversation about these values and why participants feel they are important. If possible, write the values named on a blackboard, a whiteboard, or a posted piece of newsprint so that all can see them.

5. For the next session, ask each participant to write a story from their life or a statement that expresses a value that is important to them. This value need not have been discussed in this session, but it should be one that has been important in their lives and that they want to share with the next generations.

Third Session

1. As with the previous session, start with the opportunity to pose questions and offer thoughts left over or arising from the previous week's meeting.

2. Read aloud another example of a spiritual will, distributing printed copies first, if possible. Ask for comments on how this person has approached the task of writing a spiritual will.

3. Remind participants that they were asked to write a story or share a statement that expresses a value or a virtue that is important to them and that they wish to convey to the next generations. Give each participant an opportunity to share what they have written or to talk about what came to mind as they engaged with this assignment.

4. Pass out the following handout. Give participants an opportunity to read through it and seek clarifications, if necessary.

Session 3 Handout
Summary Guide to Writing Your Spiritual Will

A spiritual will is a personal statement about what one has learned from one's life—created for the benefit of others.

—Daniel Taylor, *Creating a Spiritual Legacy*

1. Review the questions a spiritual will might address.

What have I done in and with my life?

What have I learned?

What do I value?

What is most important in life, and how has my answer to that changed over time?

When have I been happiest or felt my life had the most meaning?

What have I learned the hard way that I want someone else to learn more easily?

What can I pass on to others that will make their lives better or easier or deeper?

2. Review stories of your life.

The ongoing stories you were born into

Stories of discovery and learning, times when you found out something about who you are or who you aspire to be

Stories that express values important to you

Stories of good times or bad times and what they mean to you now

Stories of your life that you would like others to know, to remember

3. Consider your values.

Think about the values that were expressed in the class. Which of these are important to you?

How did you come to hold them?

How have your values shaped the decisions you have made, the course your life has taken?

What values and ideals would you like to pass on to the next generations?

4. Read through sample spiritual wills that have been shared in the class or that are available on the Internet.

What ideas do they suggest for your own spiritual will?

What would you like to do that is similar to these examples?

What would you like to do that is different from them?

5. Then just start writing!

Don't worry about the order you say things in. They can be rearranged. Start with what's in your mind now and see where it takes you. Let yourself be surprised.

Fourth Session

This is what the sessions up to this point have been aiming toward. Invite participants to take turns sharing their drafts of their spiritual wills. (Some participants may not have written an actual document. In that case, ask them to offer some thoughts about their legacy: what they would want the next generations to know about them and what has been important to them.)

After each presentation, take time for questions and thoughts in response to what has been shared.

Conclude this session with a conversation about what participants have gotten from this series of meetings. Also invite suggestions they may have for future sessions, either on this topic or on others.

You might conclude with a reading. I like the following:

Look to this day!
For it is life, the very life of life.
In its brief course lie all the verities
And realities of your existence:
    The bliss of growth,
    The glory of action
    The splendor of beauty;
For yesterday is but a dream,
And tomorrow is only a vision;
But today, well lived, makes every yesterday
A dream of happiness
And every tomorrow a vision of hope.
Look well, therefore, to this day.
—Attributed to Kalidasa

Acknowledgments

The primary sources for this book are conversations with people in their senior years. I have done more than fifty formal interviews, and I have also drawn from informal exchanges with seniors both in the retirement community where I am chaplain and in other communities I have participated in. We have talked about challenges and opportunities, good times and heartaches, joys and concerns in addressing the challenges of our lives today and in anticipating the next stages. These talks have been remarkable: candid, insightful, moving, often funny and filled with details of "the stuff of life." To those who have let me into their lives, I offer my thanks and my admiration.

I am tempted to label these seniors "ordinary" to distinguish them from the celebrities of our fame-obsessed era. These are people who have pursued their lives outside of the public spotlight, by and large. They have lived conscientiously; they have struggled; they have realized accomplishments and endured failures; they have brought children into the world and tried to guide them by what they find to be good and true. These are people who have tried to live with integrity and have sought to leave something of value behind for the next generations. They have played their parts in the ever-unfolding drama of the human story. So although they have lived outside of the spotlight, there is nothing ordinary about these people. They have lived with courage and hope, which is the most that can be asked of any of us.

Thank you to the professionals in the field of aging I talked with who helped orient me: Chip Warner, Jeff Watson, Michelle Glodeck, Jason Longwell, Fiona Divecha, Katie Garber, Bob Ritzen, and Gary Hibbs. Thank you also to Riderwood Village in Silver Spring, Maryland, where I serve as a chaplain, for providing an open and affirming environment in which such conversations could take place.

My gratitude and appreciation to my editors at Skinner House, Marshall Hawkins, Mary Benard, and Shoshanna Green, who patiently guided me through the process of producing this book, offering support and skillful edits. To my associates in the Pastoral Ministries Office at Riderwood Village, who demonstrate how those representing different faith communities may work together and how our diversity enriches each other. To my colleagues in the Unitarian Universalist ministry who form a community that grounds me and offers a context of wisdom and renewal. And to my wife, Amy Dibner, who has been with me at every turn of this journey, giving insight and love.

Bruce T. Marshall,
Silver Spring, Maryland